Cats in Cross Stitch

Cats in Cross Stitch

Sally Harman

The Reader's Digest Association, Inc.
Pleasantville, N. Y. • Montreal

A Reader's Digest Book
Edited and Produced by Michael O'Mara Books Limited

This book is dedicated to all cats
but in particular to Penny, Smudge, Hobbes, Cleo,
Ali, Lucky, Softy, Misty, Ellie, Juliet, Krystal,
Maya, Archie, (last but never least) Elle, and all their
respective owners, especially Tiffany.

Photography by Helen Pask
Book Design by Clive Dorman & Co.

Library of Congress Cataloging in Publication Data
Harman, Sally
        Cats in cross stitch / Sally Harman.
             p.   cm.
        ISBN 0–89577–917–X
        1. Cross-stitch—Patterns.   2. Cats in art.   I. Title.
        TT778.C76H364   1997
        746.44'3041—dc20   96-25411

Printed and bound in Hong Kong

Contents

Foreword

I was very pleased to be asked to write a foreword for this book. Cats have always been favorites of mine. They strike me as being very well organized – they love their creature comforts, warmth, luxurious surroundings and, of course, good food. If these are supplied in adequate quantities, the owner is rewarded with a loving faithful friend.

Our own cat, Penny, a tortoise-shell, had a bad start in life by being abandoned in an apartment in a back street in London. Thankfully the neighbors heard her cries and called an animal rescue group to free her. Penny was in a pitiful state and for a while we were not sure if she would live. She spent a couple of weeks in the hospital before being adopted by my wife who fell in love with her. Once she came home, she never looked back. Being a typical tortoise-shell, she has a mind of her own and is boss in our house. She still shows some signs of insecurity and needs a cuddle if her routine is upset. Cats in general are lovely animals to treat when they are ill as they respond so well to tender loving care and nursing.

Although I have a tortoise-shell my favorite cats are ginger. They are so handsome to look at and nearly always have a very friendly temperament. We had a ginger tom in the hospital recently that had fallen over seventy feet and broken both front legs. Within less than a week of the operation to repair them, he was up on his feet and greeting everybody who came near with the loudest purr you have ever heard. We were unable to find his owners, but it was a joy to see him adopted by a family with a garden. The last I heard of him he was fully recovered and climbing trees with glee. Fortunately, as he has grown older he has learned to exercise caution and can negotiate his way down safely.

I am sure that those who buy this book will have many hours of enjoyment. Cats are beautiful creatures and the designs in these pages do them full justice.

Introduction

Cats are truly magnificent creatures and this book is a celebration of their beauty, charm, and intelligence, as well as their fortitude in the face of adversity. The cats featured have all come into contact with animal rescue groups for a number of different reasons.

The *Getting Started* section provides clear information regarding various fabrics, threads, stitches, and techniques used in cross stitch. In addition, professional tips have been included, where appropriate, in order to give the reader a better understanding of certain aspects of cross stitch. It is intended that this will help the readers who may wish to produce a design based on their own cat, having first tried some of the charted projects.

As well as making the designs accessible to the beginner, the author has taken care to present work which will appeal at all needlework skill levels. Innovative ideas have also been included in the book. For example, ideas for a coffeepot cover, a clock, a photograph album, and a christmas stocking are included alongside more familiar applications of cross stitch work. As well as providing a colored chart and full instructions for each project, the author has added a footnote with alternative suggestions for working the design. On page 68, one of the alternative suggestions has been stitched and is illustrated alongside the original version, which was first featured in *All About Cats* magazine. The alternative is worked in cross stitch using wool and large-holed tapestry canvas so that, with the addition of a simple checkered border, the 4 x 6 in picture becomes a 14 in square cushion.

The final part of the book provides full instructions for creating a professional finish to the stitched pieces. Readers who usually pass items for framing on to others, or only make the occasional greeting card, will not be daunted by the information given in this section. It is intended that they will be encouraged to expand the range of their work by using pre-purchased items with cross stitch inserts, such as glass paperweights, box lids and clock mechanisms or by making book covers. This book can therefore provide a stepping-stone to adopting a more adventurous and creative approach to cross stitch work.

Getting Started

Cross stitch continues to increase in popularity, so many readers of this book will be new to the craft. *Getting Started* will therefore be a useful guide for the beginner, but the more experienced stitcher may also find the information below helpful.

FABRICS

It is possible to work cross stitch on a wide variety of fabrics as well as paper, plastic and netting. However, this book concentrates on the more familiar ones which are readily available in needlework retailers and via mail order suppliers.

Aida

The easiest fabric to use is Aida cloth, an evenweave fabric with clearly defined stitch holes, designed both for ease of work and counting of stitches or spaces. Its regular nature ensures that all your stitches will be evenly sized and thus the design will not be distorted. It comes in a variety of "count" sizes. The count number refers to the number of stitches per inch which it provides. Therefore, the larger the count, the smaller the stitch. Aida is also available in a wide range of colors and in a new non-fraying format, Aida Plus.

Linen

The comment made about count sizes needs further clarification when considering linen counts. For example, a 28-count linen can be used as a direct substitute for a 14-count Aida since conventionally cross stitch on linen is worked over a pair of the linen threads, making 14 stitches to the inch. The advantage of linen, besides its high quality appearance, is that it provides flexibility so that some greater detail may be achieved in parts of a design by working the stitches over single threads rather than over pairs of threads. It also allows a very small piece of work to be stitched with a considerable amount of detail, as in the case of the pen holder (page 56). However, linen is more difficult to use than Aida cloth because the fabric's threads move easily, increasing the chance of distortion. Stitchers need to take care when carrying threads across the back of their work because of linen's more transparent nature.

Tapestry (Needlepoint) Canvas

Like the other fabrics, this comes in various count sizes, usually referred to as holes per inch (hpi). Mono canvas has a single thread between each hole; double thread has two threads, usually interlocked, to reduce canvas thread movement. The canvas used for the black-and-white cat cushion is double thread. The larger holes are used for stitching... not the smaller holes created by canvas threads overlapping.

THREADS

In the same way that various fabrics can be used for cross stitch, a wide variety of threads can also be used – everything from the finest silk floss to ribbon, raffia, or string. The threads you will find in this book are the more conventional ones and again are readily available from good needlework stores and suppliers.

DMC Six Strand Embroidery Floss

This is a most useful embroidery thread. It is a loosely twisted cotton thread with six strands and a high-luster finish. It is best used in lengths no longer than 18 in (45 cm) and, for the designs in this book, it is divided and used as either 1, 2 or 3 strands. After cutting the required length, the two best ways to divide up the six strands are as follows:

(i) Grasp the middle of the skein's length and gently pull away, one at a time, the number of threads required; or

(ii) Hold one end of the length of the skein very firmly with one hand and with the other, find the tip of an individual strand. Holding the other strands tightly, pull the strand through your gripping fingers.

After pulling out the required strands, put their ends together so they can be used together and threaded as one thread.

DMC Medicis Wool

This is a beautiful soft 2-ply yarn of fine wool which is extremely useful for any piece of cross stitch which is likely to be exposed to frequent handling or dust when made up into a finished item. It can be substituted for stranded embroidery thread. Medicis wool is also a popular choice for crewel work. Again, use lengths no longer than 18 in (45 cm).

DMC Flower Thread

This is a non-mercerized cotton with a matte finish. It comes in a wide range of colors; one strand of flower thread is roughly equivalent to two strands of stranded floss.

DMC Tapestry Wool

This 4–ply yarn is coarser than Medicis wool and is suitable for the cross stitch cushion, although it is more usually used for half-cross stitch. Use lengths of 18 in (45 cm) or less.

DMC Metallic Thread

This can be used as the equivalent of a single strand of stranded embroidery thread, but it can also be used in double, triple or, with difficulty, quadruple lengths. Alternatively, for very fine work, it can be untwisted and divided into its component three strands. In this book, however, it is used straight from the reel and two lengths of it are stitched together and used as one thread.

EQUIPMENT

For very small pieces of work minimum equipment is required. For small projects worked on Aida cloth, the use of an embroidery hoop is a matter of personal choice. For larger pieces of work a hoop is recommended, but is by no means compulsory if you feel it hampers your working and you can stitch neatly without one. However, continual direct handling of fabric not only increases the chance of your work getting dirty but it also breaks down the structure of the fabric's sizing, which is there to retain the relative stiffness, and, thereby, the shape of the fabric.

Embroidery Hoops

These are made in various sizes and the smaller ones are easier to handle. If working a larger piece, however, it is better to use an appropriate hoop or frame. The size of the fabric you are working on will be a guide to the most appropriate hoop to use. In order to fit a hoop, a piece of fabric must be larger than the hoop's diameter.

If you have a design which you think is likely to be in an embroidery hoop for a long time, cover the fabric with a similar-sized piece of either paper or thin cotton (muslin is very good for this purpose) and then fit the fabric and its covering into the hoop together. Carefully expose the area to be stitched by tearing or cutting the protective paper or muslin. This serves two purposes. It minimizes the damage done by the hoop and it keeps the unstitched area of the fabric clean, avoiding the need to wash it after stitching. Paper is obviously more readily available than muslin but the noise made by rustling paper when handling your hoop can be distracting!

Rectangular Frames

If your fabric is too big for an embroidery hoop then you may want to use a rectangular frame. Scroll frames are useful for this purpose and plastic quilting frames are also worth considering. An old picture frame also can be put into service. If it is a very old frame, bind around it with cloth tape to protect your fabric.

Needles

Tapestry needles are blunt so that they do not split the thread of either the fabric or stitches already worked. The needles come in different sizes in either a single packet with a range of sizes or packets containing needles of one size only. I find it useful to have several needles so that if I do not use all of a length of thread in one area of stitching, that needle can be put to one side awaiting the need for that color again. This avoids unthreading and re-threading yarn.

Thimble

Because a tapestry needle is blunt, it is not essential to use a thimble for cross stitch. I personally cannot work using a thimble, but if you are used to working with one, then continue to do so.

Air-soluble Pens

These are wonderfully useful for a variety of purposes. For example, you can use one to draw lines across and down the center of a piece of fabric prior to stitching to make it easier to locate the center and avoid the need for basting stitches which would later have to be removed. The pens usually give a purple line which will fade after a short period of time if your fabric has a large amount of dressing in its finish. Other fabrics, such as linen, will often hold the colored lines for several days – so be warned if you want to complete a gift in a hurry! These inks can, however, damage some fabrics over time. Basting stitches are less convenient but won't harm the fabric.

It is most important that you do not confuse this type of pen with embroidery marker pens (which often also give a purple line) as these are permanent or semi-permanent.

Translucent Graph Paper

This is available in a variety of sizes to correspond with cross stitch fabric and tapestry canvas counts. You can produce your own chart by placing it over a photograph or picture you wish to stitch. It will help translate the image into squares. You will find it useful if you wish to substitute other cats' faces in the clock design.

Scissors

A pair of small embroidery scissors with pointed blades is vital for the clean cutting of thread and also comes in handy for unpicking any stitches worked in error. A larger pair of sharp scissors is helpful for cutting fabric.

TECHNIQUES

Preparing your Fabric

Cut your fabric to the required size. After cutting the fabric I have always found it beneficial to remove any fold creases prior to stitching or placing the fabric in an embroidery hoop. You will usually have to iron a piece after stitching, but sometimes the fold creases can prove to be extremely obstinate and I prefer to tackle them with a wet cloth and a medium-hot iron without any stitches being present.

Mark the center of your fabric by either drawing lines with an air-soluble pen or stitching lines of basting stitch. These lines should be midway along each edge and go to the midpoint of the opposite edge. Where they cross is the middle of your fabric. The midpoint of the chart can be found by following the line down from the midpoint arrows marked on the chart. Mount your fabric on a hoop or frame if using one.

Organizing your Threads

Having prepared your fabric you may find it helpful to organize your threads on a yarn holder. One way to do this is to count the number of colors to be used and cut a piece of thin acid-free cardboard to a suitable length. Allow ½ in (1 cm) for each color plus an inch (2.5 cm) at the top and bottom. The piece of cardboard should be approximately 2 in (5 cm) wide (see diagram below).

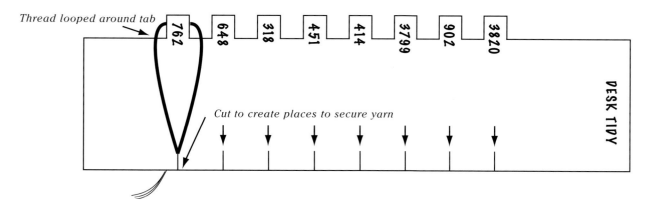

Thread looped around tab 762 648 318 451 414 3799 902 3820

Cut to create places to secure yarn

DESK TIDY

To make the yarn holder, cut one of the long sides of the cardboard to give the pattern shown above. On the opposite long side, cut ½ in (1 cm) into the cardboard opposite the midpoint of each protruding tab. You can write the color number of the thread in pencil on the tab (pencil allows you to re-use the same cardboard for another project). Keep the colors in the order they appear on the chart key so that you can find them easily. Cut a length of each color, fold each one in half in turn, and loop the doubled length around the tab, securing the ends by pulling them through the slit opposite. You can also write the title of the project on the end of the cardboard so that if you are stitching more than one piece of work at a time, you do not confuse the required threads. This allows you to keep your sorted skeins neat and clean.

Using a Chart

The charts in this book are given in color, but because they are worked on different-sized fabrics it is important to remember that *the size of the chart is not necessarily the size of the finished design.* Unless otherwise stated, each colored square represents one stitch worked over one square of Aida cloth or two threads of linen. Lines of backstitch are marked in narrow lines and half cross stitch is indicated by a half-colored square.

Once you find the center points of your fabric and charts, you are ready to work the design. Some books recommend that you count up from the center of your fabric and the chart, so that you work the design from the top downward. This minimizes the handling and any contact with stitches already made, but I find it a slightly boring method and prefer to work from the center

outward so that I am free to work in any direction I desire from the center point. The main advantage of working from the center is that you can be sure of getting the correct position on the fabric for your work. (You can always work from the midway horizon downward and then turn your work upside down to complete the other half.) Whichever way you prefer to work, you will find it helpful to stitch all white areas last.

THE STITCHES

Beginning and Ending Threads

It is important for you to know how to begin and end your threads. To start stitching, tie a knot in one end of your thread. Insert the needle down into the front of the fabric 1 in (2.5 cm) away from where you are making your first stitch and in the direction you will be working. *The knot should be on the front of your work.* Bring the needle up into the first stitch hole and then work your first stitches toward the knot. When you have completed five or six stitches, look at the back of your work. The thread between the knot and your first stitch should be held secure by the backs of the stitches. If it is, turn your work over again and hold the knot firmly, away from the fabric. Cut off the knot with sharp scissors. If the thread between the knot and first stitch is not secure, continue stitching until it is. To finish off a thread, take it to the reverse side of your work and carefully pull it through the back of nearby stitches.

Cross Stitch

Bring the needle up at 1, down at 2, up at 3 and down at 4 (A).

Make sure that all top diagonals are worked in the same direction. Complete each stitch one at a time (A), rather than working a line of half crosses and doubling back to make full crosses (B). (This ensures that the cross "sits" well in the fabric and reduces the chance of distortion.)

Try to maintain an even tension in your work. If it is too loose, it will look untidy and if it is too tight, your fabric may pucker and end up being distorted in shape.

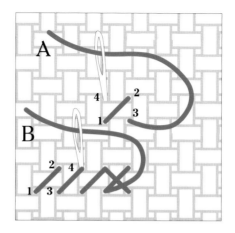

Backstitch

Bring the needle up at 1, down at 2, up at 3 and continue as required.

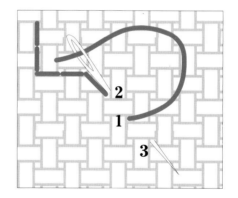

French Knots

Bring the needle up to where you wish to make the knot. Hold the thread taut in your left hand, needle in your right (or *vice versa* if left-handed). Place the needle behind the taut thread, twisting the needle round the thread twice. Push the needle back down into the fabric very close to where it came up and, keeping the thread taut, slowly take the needle to the reverse side of your work.

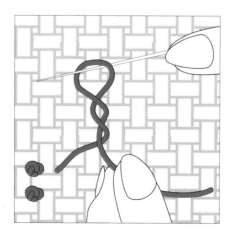

Picture Frames and Mats

If you are a cat owner or cat lover you will
no doubt have accumulated several cat pictures
and greetings cards featuring them. Why not
stitch these simple-to-make mats and picture
frames so you can display some of your
favorites rather than have them tucked away in
a drawer? They also make a very suitable gift for
a cat-loving friend. You can personalize the
frames and mats by adding the cat's name and
the year the photograph was taken.

MATERIALS

Paw Print Picture Mat, stitched area 8 x 6⅛ in (20.5 x 15.5 cm)

Sheet of Aida Plus in white or ivory
DMC Six Strand Embroidery Floss in 3042 Pale Purple or suitable alternative to match your photograph
Suitable picture frame
Masking tape

Mice Picture Mat, stitched area 5⅛ in (13 cm) square

Sheet of Aida Plus in white or ivory
DMC Six Strand Embroidery Floss in 613 Stone plus two suitable shades to match the photograph (334 Blue and 436 Ginger were used for the mat illustrated)
Suitable picture frame
Masking tape

Rectangular Picture Frame, stitched area 6⅛ x 8¼ in (15.5 x 21 cm)

Sheet of Aida Plus in light gray
DMC Six Strand Embroidery Floss as follows:

472	Lime Green
3820	Gold
3827	Pale Ginger
3776	Ginger
666	Red
646	Dark Gray
648	Gray

Double-faced adhesive tape
Matting, cut to fit the finished frame

Square Picture Frame, stitched area 6⅛ in (15.5 cm) square

Sheet of Aida Plus in red
DMC Six Strand Embroidery Floss as for Picture Frame No. 1 but substituting 793 Blue for 666 Red
Double-faced adhesive tape
Matting, cut to fit the finished frame

You will also need a tapestry needle, size 24, for each of these projects.

WORKING THE CROSS STITCH

Prepare the sheet of Aida Plus by marking out the area needed to display the photograph. The best way to do this is to measure your photograph and then create a paper template which is ½ in (1.25 cm) smaller in both length and width. Place this template in the center of the Aida Plus and mark the corner positions of the paper with two large stitches in each corner. (You can use an air-soluble pen if you prefer.) DO NOT CUT THE AIDA PLUS AT THIS STAGE. Begin working the chart, working around the frame or mat.

Use two strands for the picture mats.

Use three strands for the picture frames except for the 3820 Gold which is worked using a single strand.

Below: Key for Rectangular Picture Frame

𝒦ey

DMC numbers underlined indicates backstitch

	472		3827	⊟	666	T	648
	3820	‖	3776	↑	646		

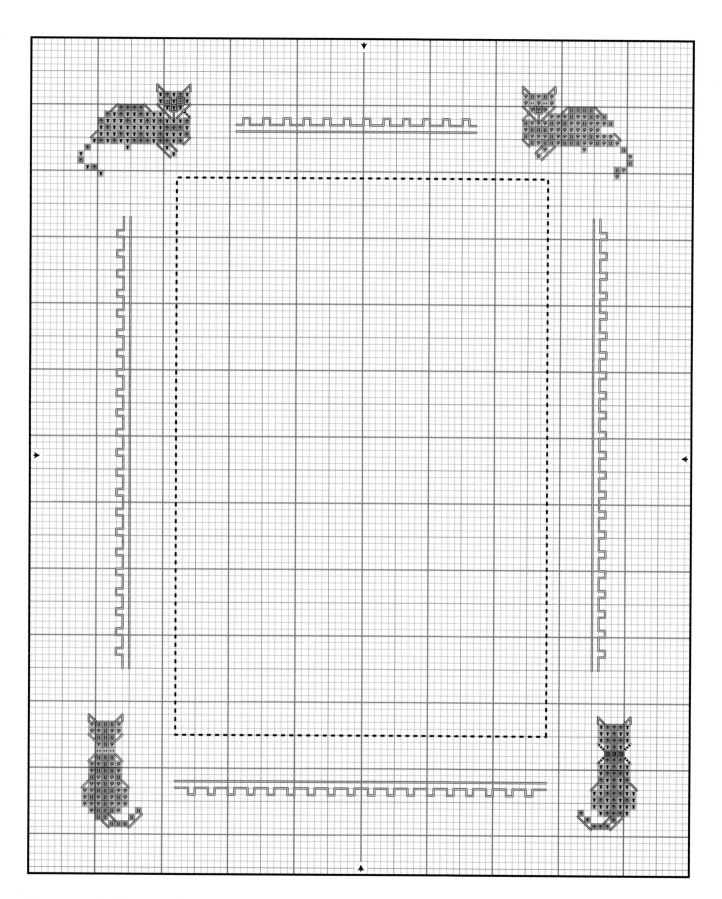

Rectangular Picture Frame

FINISHING THE WORK

Picture Mats

Using a pair of small-bladed sharp scissors, carefully cut out the central area, following the lines of the Aida Plus from corner mark to corner mark. Place the photograph in position and attach to the back of the Aida Plus using masking tape. Trim the outer edges of the Aida Plus if required. Place the mat and photograph in the frame.

Picture Frames

Using a pair of small-bladed sharp scissors, carefully cut out the central area, following the lines of the Aida Plus. Trim the outer edges of the Aida, to adjust the size and/or straighten the edges. Trim your mat, if necessary, so that it is the same size as the Aida Plus. Attach strips of double-faced adhesive tape to the wrong side of the Aida Plus, but *to side edges and bottom edge only*. When positioning the strips, place them ⅜ in (1cm) away from the central area to allow space to slide in the photograph. Remove the protective strips and carefully place the Aida Plus on the mat. If a stand-up frame is desired, attach a second piece of board to the back of the mat, scoring it lightly where it is to be bent. For a hanging frame, attach picture mounts to the back of the mat and thread with picture cord or wire. Slide the photograph into position and display or hang the finished work.

ALTERNATIVE SUGGESTIONS FOR THE DESIGN

The individual motifs can be used in a variety of combinations to decorate a number of small items, such as the back of a purse-sized mirror or the Aida strip on specially manufactured baby bibs.

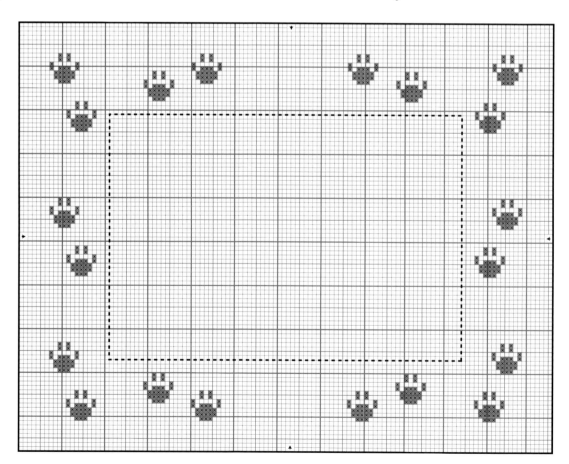

Paw Print Picture Mat

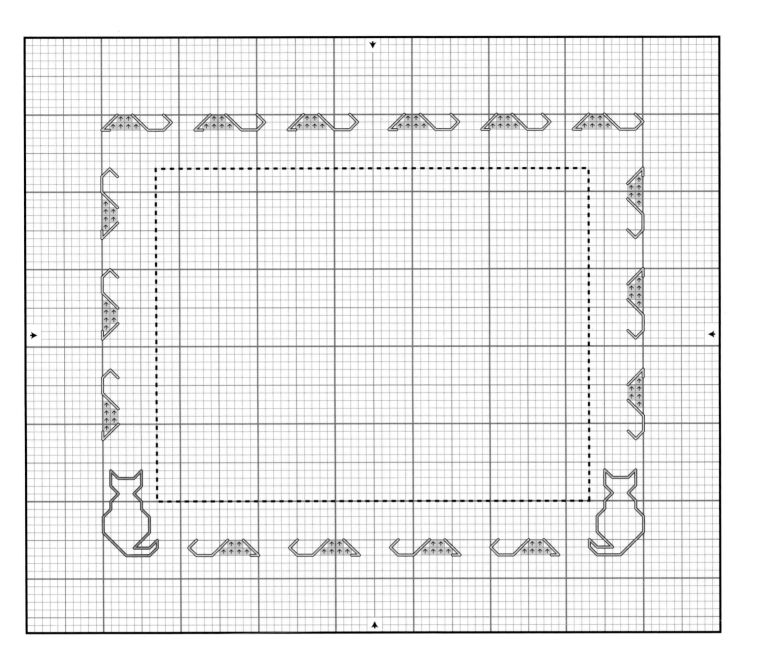

Mice Picture Mat

Key

DMC numbers underlined
indicates backstitch

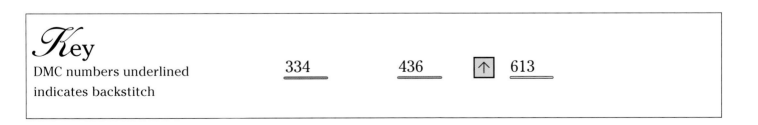

334   436   ↑ 613

Christmas Sock and Stocking

Some cats think every day should be Christmas. You can make this festive time more special by making these present holders. The sock will hold a new catnip toy, ping-pong ball, and small bag of treats. The stocking is for the more demanding cat who expects to be indulged with a little extra!

MATERIALS

Red Sock, stitched area $4\frac{3}{8}$ x $1\frac{5}{8}$ in (11 x 4 cm)

Zweigart Decorative Band 2 in (5 cm) wide, in green, 11 in (27.5 cm) long

DMC Six Strand Embroidery Floss as follows:

310	Black
BLANC	White
3820	Gold
606	Red
553	Purple
807	Blue
964	Turquoise

Sock fabric of your choice and matching cotton thread

Tapestry needles, size 24

Sock template enlarged by 400% and traced on to thin poster board

Green Stocking, stitched area $5\frac{1}{4}$ x $1\frac{1}{2}$ in (13.5 x 4 cm)

Zweigart Decorative Band, $2\frac{1}{4}$ in (5.75 cm) wide, in red, 13 in (33 cm) long

DMC Six Strand Embroidery Floss as follows:

353	Pink
BLANC	White
807	Blue
989	Green
904	Dark Green
3031	Brown
841	Dark Mushroom
543	Flesh

Stocking fabric of your choice and matching cotton thread

Tapestry needles, size 24

Stocking template enlarged by 400% and traced on to thin poster board

WORKING THE CROSS STITCH

Following the chart, beginning ½ in (1.25 cm) away from the right-hand end of the strip, with the far right edges of the design.

Use two strands throughout.

FINISHING THE WORK

Cut out two pieces of either sock or stocking fabric, using the appropriate enlarged template (see diagram below). Sew the sock/stocking, right sides together, using a ½ in (1.25 cm) seam allowance. Trim the curved edges and turn right side out. Fold the hem allowance over at the top edge so that the raw edge hangs over the front of the sock/stocking. Press the hem allowance and seam. Attach the hanging ribbon to the hem allowance at the opposite corner to the toe. Sew the two ends of the band together using a ½ in (1.25 cm) seam, checking that it fits the sock/stocking top edge. Slip stitch to the sock/stocking top, covering the hem allowance at the top edge.

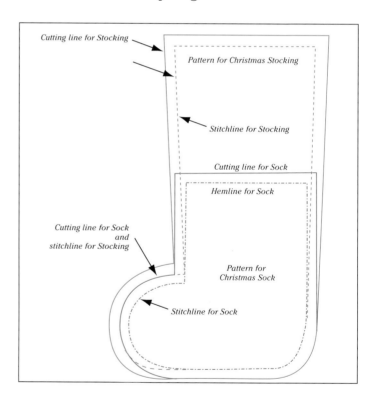

ALTERNATIVE SUGGESTION FOR THE DESIGN

Both these designs can be adapted for Christmas cards.

Opposite top: Christmas Sock
Opposite bottom: Christmas Stocking

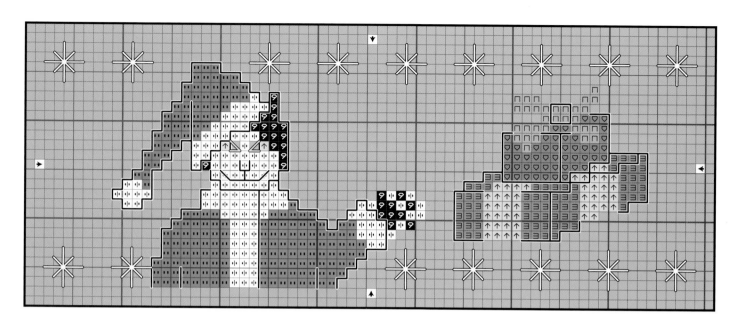

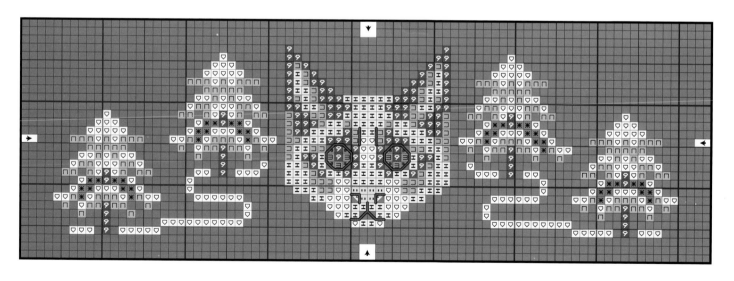

Greeting Cards

Cats are very patient creatures and fascinated by water so these two characteristics have been combined in this design. These two versions of the same design can be used either as a general greeting card, a get well card, or a good luck greeting. If you are feeling adventurous, vary the colors of the wishing well, flowers, or cat to suit your taste.

MATERIALS

For design, stitched area 2 ⅝ x 3 ½ in
   (6.5 x 9 cm)

Zweigart 18-count Aida cloth in cream (for the
   white cat) or white (for the black cat),
   8 x 10 in (20.5 x 25.5 cm)

DMC Six Strand Embroidery Floss as follows:

Black Cat

310	Black
3609	Pale Violet
893	Dark Pink
340	Mauve
3013	Pale Green
320	Dark Green
350	Red
746	Cream
840	Brown
613	Dark Mushroom
3045	Golden Brown
3821	Gold
3046	Pale Gold

White Cat

BLANC	White
727	Lemon
973	Yellow
742	Orange
471	Pale Green
3347	Green
996	Turquoise
921	Terra Cotta
407	Dusty Pink
840	Brown
613	Mushroom
3046	Pale Gold
371	Green Gold

Tapestry needles, size 24
Blank card in dark green or cream
Double-faced adhesive tape

WORKING THE CROSS STITCH

The same chart can be used to make both of
the cards illustrated. Follow the chart, beginning in the center of the Aida and working
outward. If stitching the white cat version,
stitch the cat last.

*Use two strands throughout. Add backstitch,
using one strand of 840, for the outer edge of
the White Cat.*

FINISHING THE WORK

See the section *Finishing Your Work* page 122
for details on fixing your stitched work to the
card.

ALTERNATIVE SUGGESTION
FOR THE DESIGN

These cats can also be used to decorate the
oval insert in the address book (page 32).

Key DMC numbers underlined indicates backstitch

	White Cat	Black Cat		White Cat	Black Cat
⊡	BLANC	310	⊐	921	746
■■	727	3609	☰	407	840
▽	973	893	↑	840	613
⊟	742	340	∨	613	3045
⊓	471	3013	△	3046	3821
✳	3347	320	◪	371	3046
•◦•	996	350			

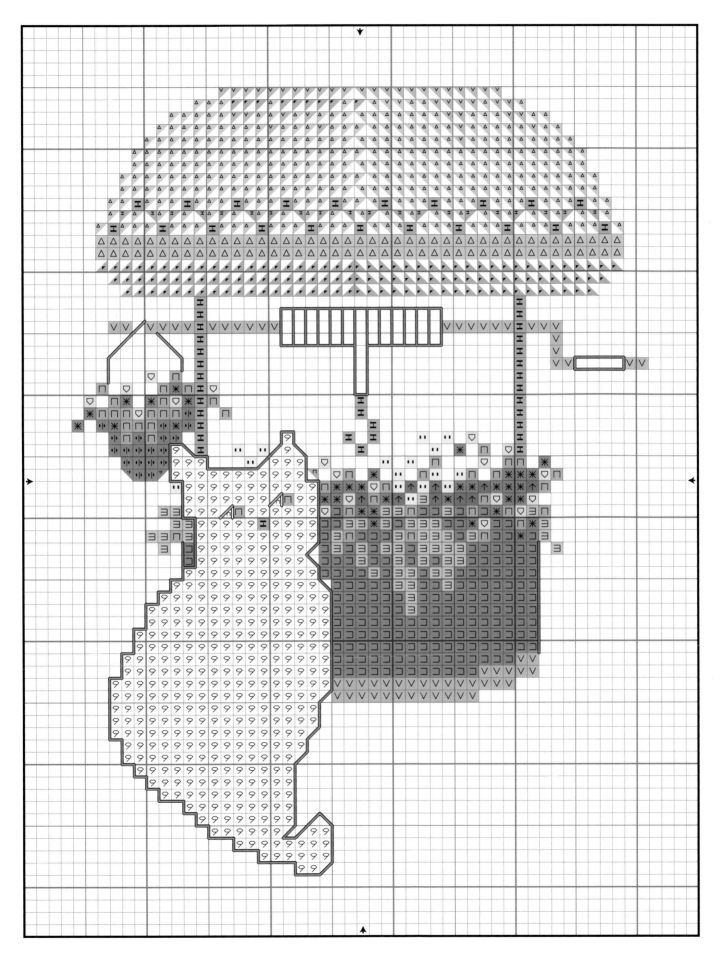

Calendar

This cat is intended to represent all cats
who live contented lives after being saved by
the animal rescue groups. This calendar
design has been worked in Medicis wool.
If desired, change the yarn colors to
suit your own decor.

MATERIALS

For design, stitched area $3\frac{5}{8}$ in (9 cm) square

Zweigart 14-count Aida cloth in emerald
   green, 9 x 11 in (23 x 28 cm)

DMC Medicis Wool as follows:

8720	Royal Blue
8995	Kingfisher Blue
8997	Pale Blue
8419	Green
8327	Yellow

DMC Tapestry needles, size 20
Blank Calendar
Picture Frame, inner measurement $4\frac{1}{2}$ x $6\frac{1}{2}$ in
   (11.5 x 16.5 cm)

WORKING THE CROSS STITCH

Follow the chart, beginning with the first
horizontal row of the check background,
which should be stitched $2\frac{1}{2}$ in (6.5 cm) from
the top edge of the fabric. Continue to work
the cat and then complete the rest of the
background.

Use one thread of Medicis wool throughout.

FINISHING THE WORK

See the section *Finishing Your Work* page 122
for details on preparing your work for framing
and other framing information.

ALTERNATIVE SUGGESTIONS FOR THE DESIGN

The design itself is square and so it can be
used to make a pincushion, or a potpourri
sachet for a room or wardrobe. A wide fabric
border can be added to make a larger cushion
for a chair or sofa.

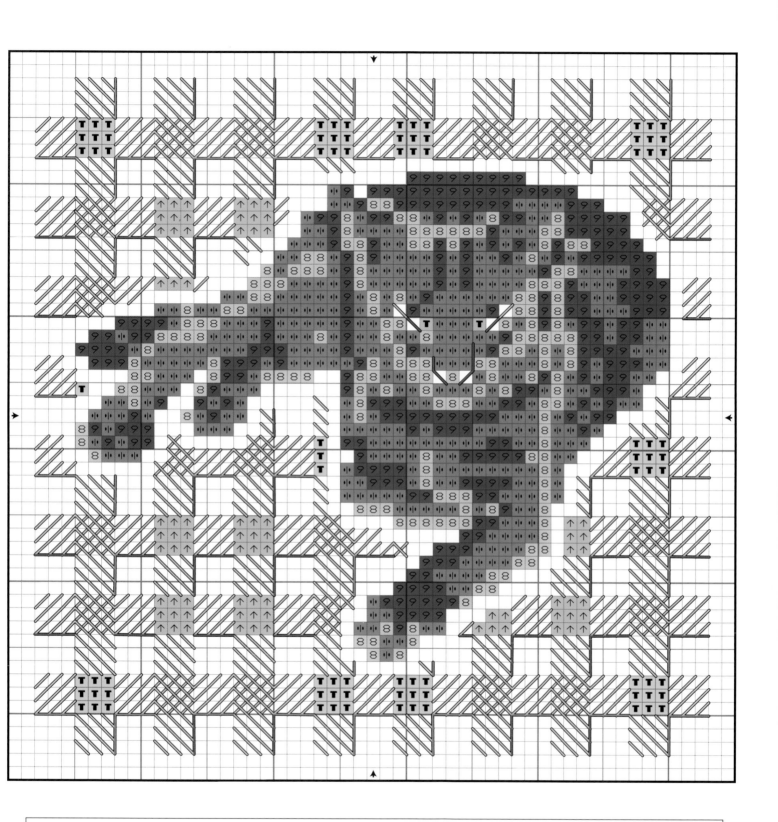

DMC numbers underlined
indicates backstitch

Symbol	DMC
9	8720
8	8997
T	8327
•‖•	8995
↑	8419

Address Book

Some kittens are so sweet and this one is just adorable! Her colors are such that she is an obvious choice to complement this address book or birthday book cover. An ideal present for any cat enthusiast.

MATERIALS

For design, stitched area 2⅛ x 3¾ in
(5.5 x 9.5 cm)

Zweigart 14-count Aida cloth in cream
9 x 11 in (23 x 28 cm)

DMC Six Strand Embroidery Floss as follows:

931	Blue
841	Dusty Pink
644	Palest Gray
3023	Pale Gray
647	Medium Gray
645	Dark Gray
535	Charcoal Gray

Tapestry needles, size 24

Address/Birthday Book or kit with
embroidery insert

WORKING THE CROSS STITCH

Follow the chart, beginning in the center of
the Aida and working outward.

Use two strands throughout.

FINISHING THE WORK

See *Finishing Your Work* page 122 for
instructions on covering a book.

ALTERNATIVE SUGGESTIONS
FOR THE DESIGN

This design can be framed to make a
delightful small picture or sent as a greeting
card, using a blank oval card.

𝒦ey

DMC numbers
underlined
indicates
backstitch

931	644	647	535
841	3023	645	

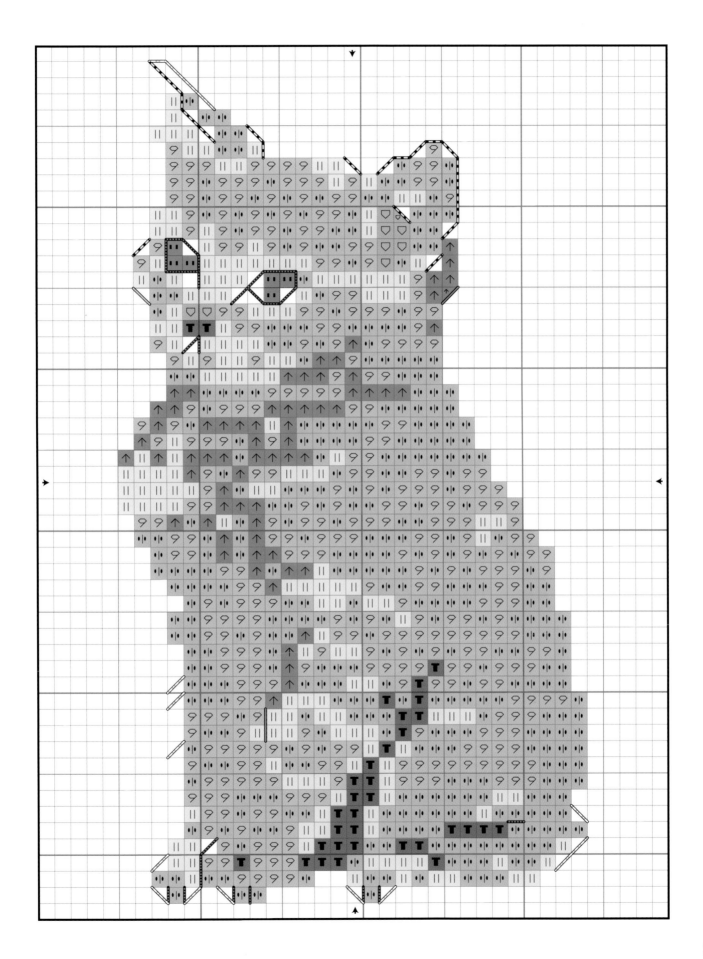

Paperweight

A paperweight is an ideal gift and this charming tortoise-shell cat surrounded by poppies makes a decorative addition to anyone's desk. Back the design with felt and add a ribbon loop to make a delightful ornament.

MATERIALS

For design, stitched area 2⅝ in (6.5 cm)
    diameter

Zweigart 18-count Aida cloth in cream, 8 in
    (20.5 cm) square

DMC Six Strand Embroidery Floss as follows:

310	Black
3371	Brown Black
3021	Dark Brown
840	Brown
613	Mushroom
3033	Palest Mushroom
822	Palest Stone
3828	Tobacco
422	Pale Tobacco
608	Orange
606	Scarlet
666	Red
3802	Purple
906	Green
472	Pale Green
758	Blush

DMC Gold metallic embroidery thread (744)
Tapestry needles, size 24
Clear glass paperweight 3½ in (9 cm)
    diameter, with a flat bottom for inserting
    embroidery

WORKING THE CROSS STITCH

Follow the chart, beginning in the center of
the Aida and working outward. Work the
backstitch around the eyes *after* completing
the other eye colors.

Use two strands throughout.

FINISHING THE WORK

See *Finishing Your Work* page 122 for
instructions on fitting a circular paperweight.

ALTERNATIVE SUGGESTIONS
FOR THE DESIGN

This design can also be framed with a circular
mount and a square frame to make a lovely
picture. A geometric border can be added to
make a potpourri holder or pincushion.

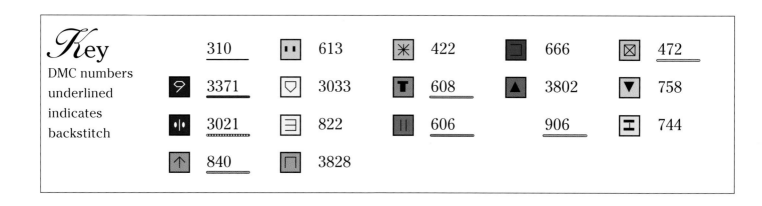

Key

DMC numbers
underlined
indicates
backstitch

	310	▫▫	613	✳	422	◩	666	⊠	472
⑨	3371	▽	3033	T	608	▲	3802	▼	758
◖▮◗	3021	⊟	822	‖	606		906	⊐	744
↑	840	◰	3828						

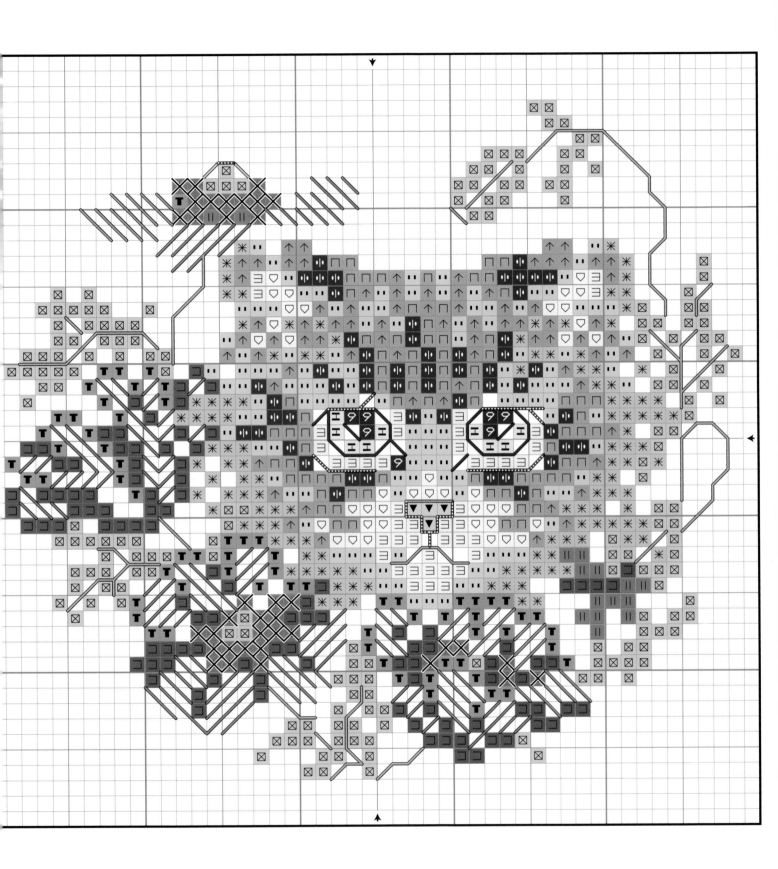

Candlescreen

Here is a cat, doing what cats do best, sleeping in a comfortable spot. This screen makes a lovely decorative feature for the home. It can be used as a backdrop for a hall table decoration, with candles or as an attractive accent on a corner shelf or dresser.

MATERIALS

For design, stitched area 3 x 4½ in
  (7.5 x 11.5 cm)

Zweigart 14-count Aida cloth in rustico
  (shade 54), 9 x 11 in (23 x 28 cm)

DMC Stranded Embroidery Floss as follows:

677	Buttermilk
746	Cream
613	Pale Mushroom
422	Gold
434	Light Brown
921	Ginger
315	Dusky Plum
3803	Purple
3768	Blue
904	Dark Green
988	Light Green
523	Pale Sage

Tapestry needles, size 24
Candlescreen kit, screen size 3½ x 5 in
  (9 x 12.5 cm)

WORKING THE CROSS STITCH

Follow the chart, beginning in the center of
the Aida and working outward.

Use two strands throughout.

FINISHING THE WORK

See *Finishing Your Work* page 122 for details of
preparing your work for framing and other
framing information.

ALTERNATIVE SUGGESTION FOR THE DESIGN

This picture will also fit inside the framed
area of the mirror shown on page 52.

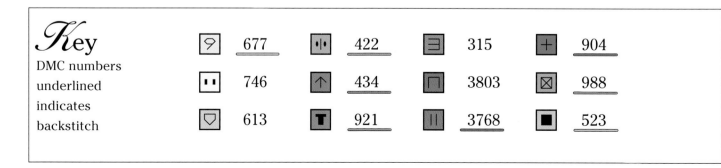

Key
DMC numbers
underlined
indicates
backstitch

♀	677	•|•	422	⊟	315	+	904
••	746	↑	434	⊓	3803	⊠	988
▽	613	T	921	⫼	3768	■	523

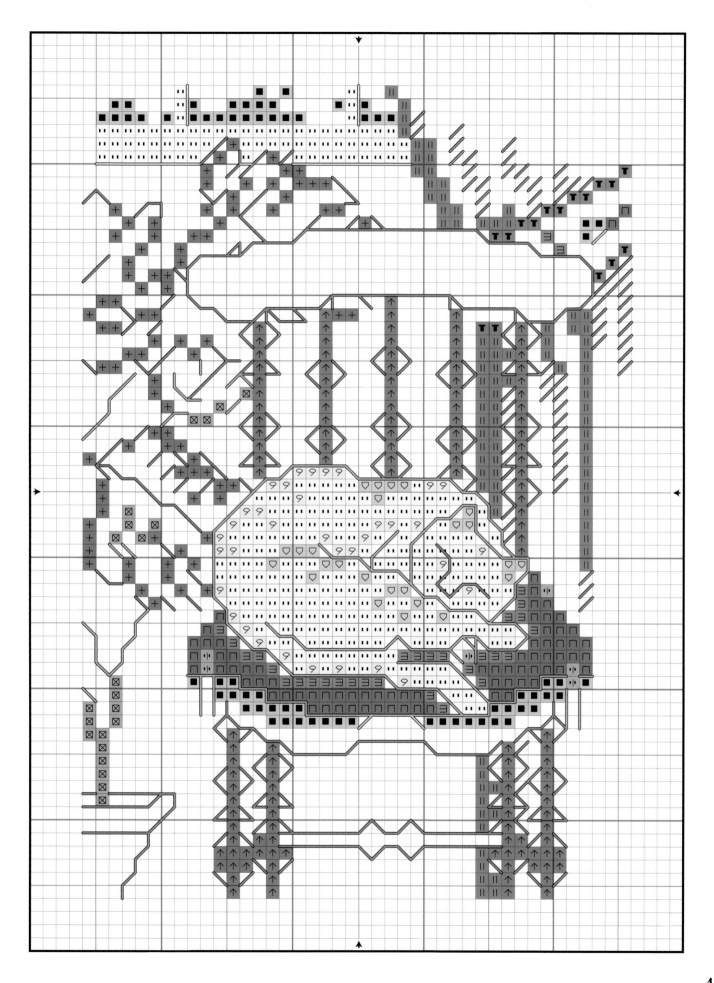

Wooden Needles & Scissors Box

· · · · · · ·

*A*re you always misplacing your scissors and needles? If so, this decorative box with two thin flat magnets hidden inside to secure its contents is the answer to your problem. This half-Persian cat decorating the inset is also used for the photograph album cover. So, if you are looking for a pair of items as a gift for someone, stitch both these projects.

MATERIALS

For design, stitched area 3 x 1⅜ in
   (7.5 x 3.5 cm)

Zweigart 18-count Aida cloth in cream,
   8 x 6 in (20.5 x 15.5 cm)

DMC Six Strand Embroidery Floss as follows:

BLANC   White
677   Buttermilk
676   Pale Ginger
436   Ginger
434   Dark Ginger
407   Dusty Pink
3821   Gold
Tapestry needles, size 24
Wooden box with embroidery insert
   3⅝ x 1⅞ in (9 x 4.5 cm)
Double-faced adhesive tape

WORKING THE CROSS STITCH

Follow the chart, beginning in the center of the Aida and working outward.

Use two strands for the cat's body. The backstitch which outlines the cat should be worked using one strand.

FINISHING THE WORK

See *Finishing Your Work* page 122 for details on attaching your finished piece to the box.

ALTERNATIVE SUGGESTION FOR THE DESIGN

Stitched on 14-count Aida to enlarge the design, this would fit horizontally into an oval blank greeting card.

𝒦ey

DMC numbers
underlined
indicates
backstitch

 434   BLANC   ▽ 677   ⊟ 676   ⊓ 436

▲ 3821   407

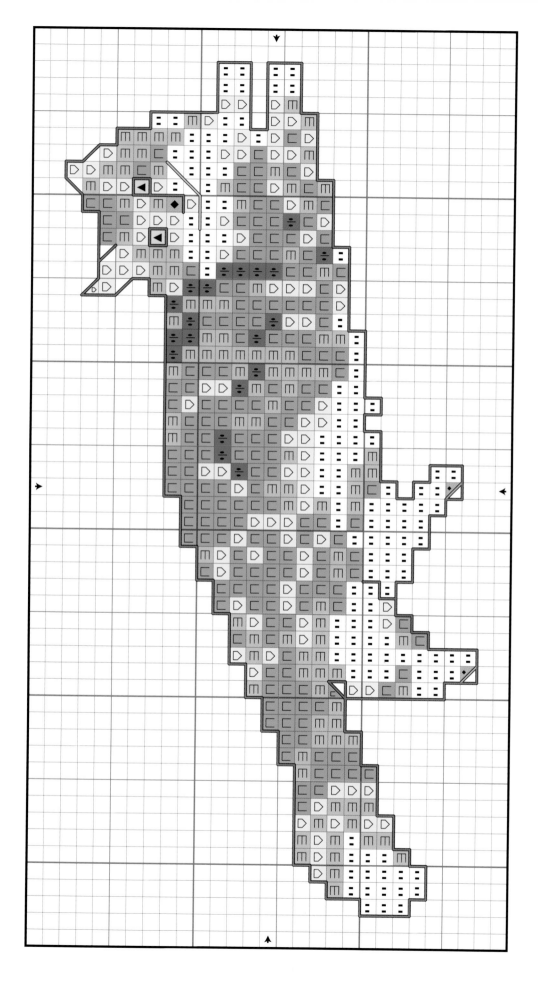

47

Silver-plated Box

Siamese cats always appear to have an air of superiority about them so it seems appropriate to use one for this box. The bargello background of muted shades is easy to work, but if you prefer, this can be omitted to give a simple elegant portrait.

MATERIALS

For design, stitched area 3½ in (9 cm) square

Zweigart 28-count linen in cream, 9 in (23 cm) square

DMC Six Strand Embroidery Floss as follows:

The Cat

799	Blue
ECRU	Ecru
3033	Pale Mushroom
841	Dark Mushroom
840	Brown
839	Medium Brown
838	Dark Brown
3371	Brown Black

The Background

3712	Rose Pink
761	Pale Pink
3823	Cream
676	Gold
320	Green
503	Turquoise Green

Tapestry needles, size 24

Silver-plated box, with embroidery insert on lid 3½ in (9 cm) square

WORKING THE CROSS STITCH

Follow the chart, beginning in the center of the linen and working outward.

Use two strands for the cat. Work the bargello-style background using one strand of each of the colors.

FINISHING THE WORK

See *Finishing Your Work* page 122 for instructions on fitting work to a circle.

ALTERNATIVE SUGGESTIONS FOR THE DESIGN

This design will fit the teapot stand on page 60. You can stitch it as given in the chart, in which case it will have an unstitched border between the design edge and the teapot stand, or you can extend the bargello-style background to fill the additional space.

With some modification to the background it can also be used for the paperweight on page 36.

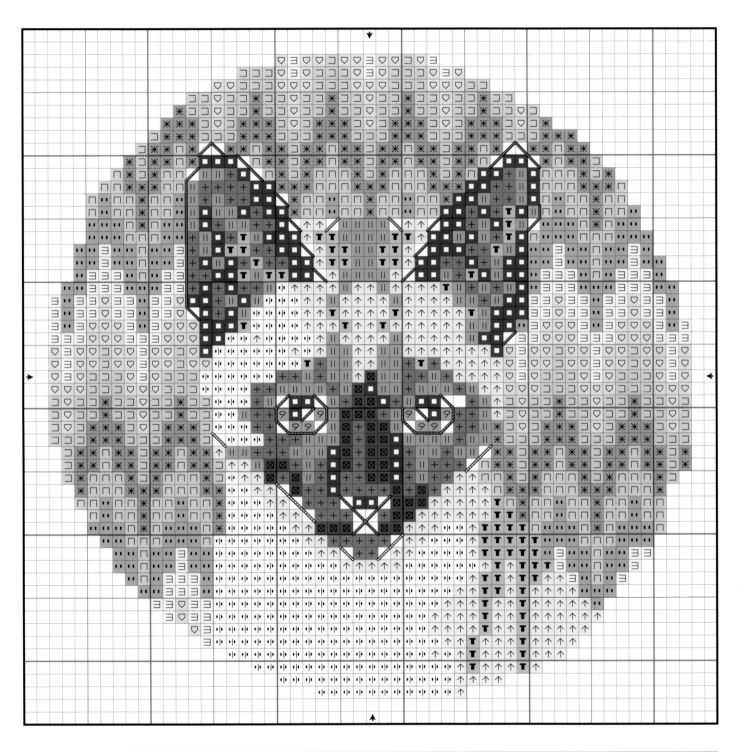

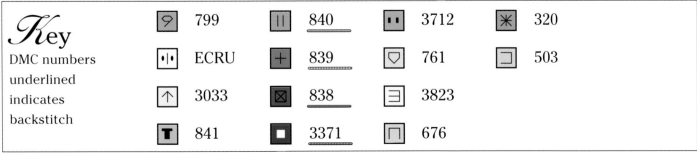

Mirror

Cats are inquisitive and this adorable kitten
will ensure you are not alone when scrutinizing
your face in this mirror. This mirror will
brighten up any room or hallway. If preferred,
the mirror can be placed partially behind a
plant or floral decoration to enhance the
plant's size and appearance.

MATERIALS

For design, stitched area 3¼ x 4⅜ in
   (8 x 11 cm)

Zweigart 18-count Aida cloth in cream,
   8 x 10 in (20.5 x 25.5 cm)

DMC Six Strand Embroidery Floss as follows:

838	Dark Brown
920	Dark Ginger
437	Pale Ginger
738	Pale Coffee
712	Cream
3033	Beige
453	Pale Gray
642	Pale Gray Brown
640	Medium Gray Brown
3787	Dark Gray Brown
523	Pale Sage

Tapestry needles, size 24

Mirror kit with embroidery insert 3½ x 5 in
   (9 x 12.5 cm)

WORKING THE CROSS STITCH

Follow the chart, beginning in the center of
the Aida and working outward.

Use two strands throughout.

FINISHING THE WORK

See *Finishing Your Work* page 122 for details of
fixing your stitched work to the framing part
of the mirror.

ALTERNATIVE SUGGESTIONS FOR THE DESIGN

This can be framed as a picture with a mat
and a larger frame. It would also be an
attractive front cover for a small notebook,
made in the same way as the photograph
album cover on page 82.

Key

DMC numbers
underlined
indicates
backstitch

Symbol	DMC	Symbol	DMC	Symbol	DMC
၅	838 (underlined)	⊟	712	⊞	640
•ı•	920 (underlined)	⊓	3033	▼	3787
ıı	437	✳	453	▲	523
▽	738	⊟	642		

Pen Holder

If you sometimes find it difficult to put pen
to paper, perhaps the authoritative stare of
this gray cat is just what you need to
act as a prompt!

MATERIALS

For design, stitched area 1¾ x 1¾ in
   (4.5 x 4.5 cm)

Zweigart 28-count linen in white, 7 in (18 cm)
   square

DMC Six Strand Embroidery Floss as follows:

3820	Gold
902	Maroon
3799	Charcoal Gray
414	Dark Gray
451	Taupe
318	Blue Gray
648	Pale Stone Gray
762	Palest Gray

Tapestry needles, size 24
Pen holder kit with embroidery insert

WORKING THE CROSS STITCH

Follow the chart, beginning in the center of
the linen and working outward.

*The whole design is worked using single
strands of floss. The cross stitch is worked over
a single thread of the linen, some of the
backstitch is worked over two strands, and the
gold edges of the book are single stitches
worked across the width of the book.*

FINISHING THE WORK

See *Finishing Your Work* page 122 for
instructions on fitting work to a circle.

ALTERNATIVE SUGGESTION FOR THE DESIGN

This can be worked on 14- or 18-count Aida
and used to decorate a box lid. If doing this,
remember to allow for the increased size of
fabric required.

Key
DMC numbers underlined
indicates backstitch

3820		9	3799	▼	451	⊓	648
902		▪▪	414	▽	318	✳	762

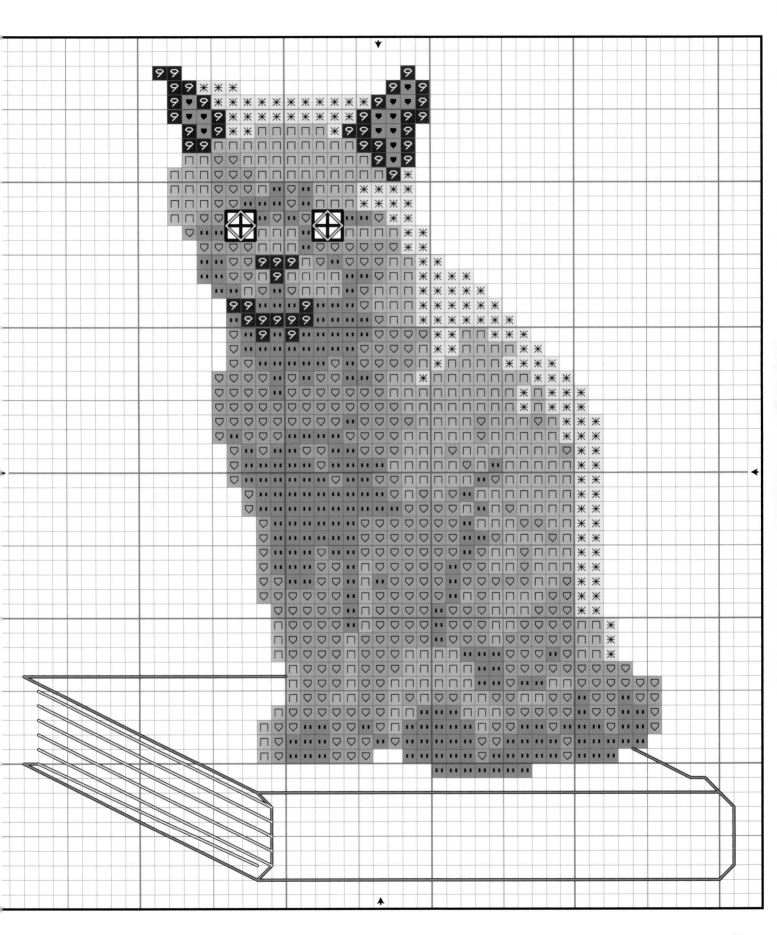

Teapot Stand

Whether you use this piece as a teapot stand or simply as a framed picture to prop up on a shelf or hang on a wall, Ellie's complacent gaze will surely bring you pleasure.

MATERIALS

For design, stitched area 3⅞ x 3¾ in
   (10 x 9.5 cm)

Zweigart 14-count Aida cloth in rustico (shade
   54), 10 in (25.5 cm) square

DMC Six Stranded Embroidery Floss as
   follows:

934	Darkest Green
471	Medium Green
3013	Sage Green
772	Pale Green
799	Medium Blue
341	Pale Blue
775	Palest Sky Blue
210	Mauve
407	Dusty Pink
738	Sand
977	Orange
3021	Dark Brown
3790	Brown
3782	Mushroom
822	Pale Mushroom
745	Palest Yellow
833	Gold

Tapestry needles, size 24
Teapot stand kit with embroidery insert
   4½ in (11.5 cm) diameter

WORKING THE CROSS STITCH

Follow the chart, beginning in the center of
the Aida and working outward.

*Use two strands throughout mixing colors where
indicated in the key.*

FINISHING THE WORK

See *Finishing Your Work* page 122 for
instructions on fitting your work to a circle.

ALTERNATIVE SUGGESTION
FOR THE DESIGN

This design can be stitched on 22-count Aida
cloth and used to decorate a box lid.

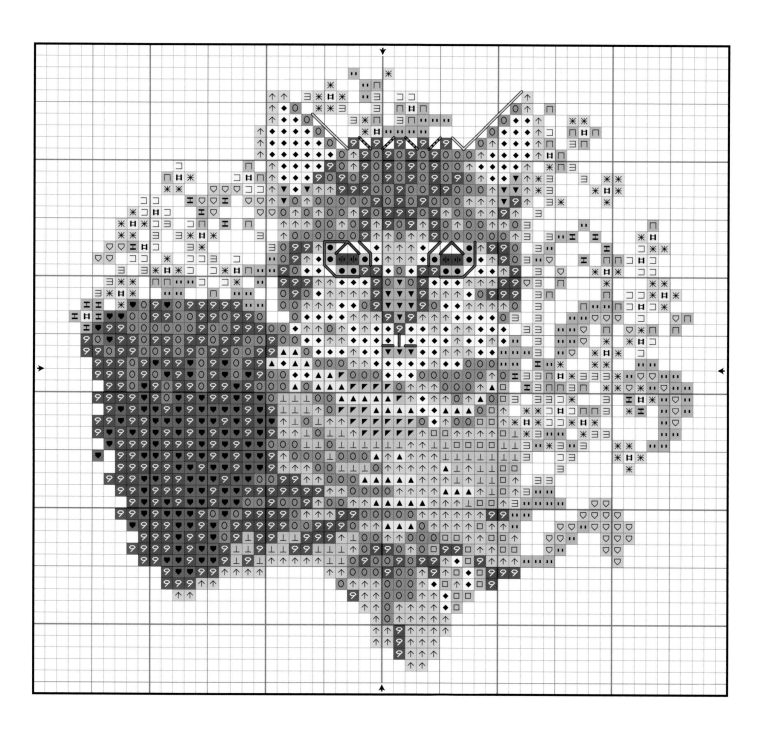

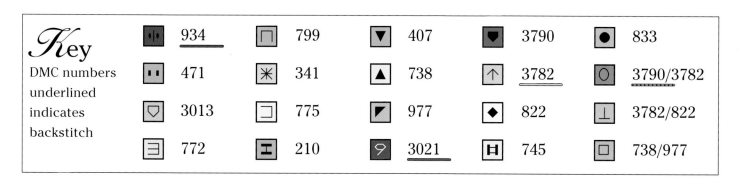

Key

DMC numbers underlined indicates backstitch

Symbol	DMC	Symbol	DMC	Symbol	DMC	Symbol	DMC	Symbol	DMC
◑	934	⊓	799	▼	407	◥	3790	●	833
▪▪	471	✳	341	▲	738	↑	3782	◓	3790/3782
▽	3013	⊐	775	◣	977	◆	822	⊥	3782/822
⊒	772	⊞	210	�9	3021	H	745	▢	738/977

Picture and Cushion

This design, based on one of my
own cats, Elle, can be used in two quite
different ways. The cross stitch picture uses
the conventional approach, but the cushion is
easy to work because cross stitch in wool is
used on large-holed canvas. Not all designs are
suitable for enlargement in this way, but here
the design and the added checkered border
combine to make a stunning cushion.

MATERIALS FOR FRAMED PICTURE

For design, stitched area 4¼ x 6¼ in
 (11 x 16 cm)

Zweigart 14-count Aida cloth in cream,
 10 x 12 in (25.5 x 31 cm)

DMC Six Strand Embroidery Floss as follows:

333	Purple
349	Red
3801	Geranium Red
950	Light Pink
948	Palest Pink
727	Pale Yellow
743	Golden Yellow
742	Dark Golden Yellow
733	Olive Green
472	Pale Green
3364	Medium Green
3346	Dark Green
611	Brown
3799	Gray Black
762	Pale Gray
ECRU	Ecru
B5200	White
310	Black

Tapestry needles, size 24

Picture mat, external measurement 7 x 9 in
 (18 x 23 cm)

Picture frame, internal measurement 7 x 9 in
 (18 x 23 cm)

WORKING THE CROSS STITCH

Follow the chart, beginning in the center of the Aida and working outward, but stitch the White last. Use backstitch in 611 for the nose and mouth, and backstitch in 733 for the top edge of the eye and far right daffodil.

Use three strands throughout the piece.

FINISHING THE WORK

See *Finishing Your Work* page 122 for details on preparing your work for framing.

MATERIALS FOR CUSHION COVER

For design, stitched area 13¾ (35 cm) square

Zweigart cotton tapestry canvas 7 hpi double
  floss in white, 19 in (48 cm) square

DMC Tapestry Wool in the following quantities:

1 skein each of:

7243	Purple
7666	Red
7106	Geranium Red
7121	Light Pink
7191	Palest Pink
7078	Pale Yellow
7726	Golden Yellow
7742	Dark Golden Yellow
7677	Olive Green
7361	Pale Green
7424	Medium Green
7384	Dark Green
7525	Brown
7624	Gray Black

3 skeins of:

7300	Pale Gray

6 skeins of:	ECRU
7 skeins of:	BLANC
7 skeins of:	NOIR

Tapestry needles, size 16

Cushion backing fabric, 15 in (38 cm) square

Zipper to match cushion backing fabric, 10 in
  (25.5 cm) in length

Cotton thread for attaching zipper and
  cushion backing

Cushion form, 14 in (35.5 cm) square

For the tassels: 3 skeins 7666 Red, 3 skeins
  7106 Geranium Red

WORKING THE CROSS STITCH

Follow the main chart, beginning in the center
of the canvas and working outward. Stitch the
BLANC *after* the ECRU background. (The
ECRU background is extended by 3 rows of
cross stitch at the top edge of the design and
2 rows at the bottom edge.) Use backstitch in
7525 for the nose and mouth, and backstitch
in 7677 for the top edge of the eye and far
right daffodil.

   Work 1 row of 7106 at each side of the cat
design, from top to bottom.

   Work 1 row of 7666 outside the rows of
7106 at each edge of the design.

   Stitch the checkered border, as shown in
the small chart, along both sides of the cat.

FINISHING THE WORK

See *Finishing Your Work* page 123 for details
on finishing the cushion and tassel-making.

ALTERNATIVE SUGGESTION
FOR THE DESIGN

In addition to the picture and cushion
illustrated, the design worked on 18-count
Aida cloth will fit into the mirror on page 52.

Top edge of cushion strip border

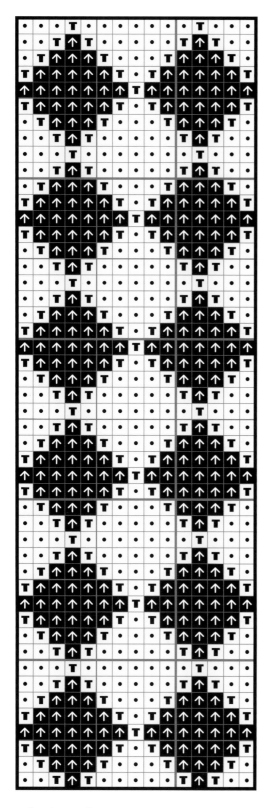

Above: Cushion Strip Border. Repeat pattern to bottom of cushion.

Key

DMC numbers underlined indicates backstitch

Framed Picture		Cushion Cover	
▦	333	▦	7243
▽	349	▽	7666
⊟	3801	⊟	7106
⊓	950	⊓	7121
✳	948	✳	7191
✕	727	✕	7078
⊞	743	⊞	7726
▼	742	▼	7742
▲	733	▲	7677
◤	472	◤	7361
▼	3364	▼	7424
◆	3346	◆	7384
●	611	●	7525
⊠	3799	⊠	7624
T	762	T	7300
•	ECRU	•	ECRU
⊐	B5200	⊐	BLANC
↑	310	↑	NOIR

Coffeepot Cover

Kittens are fascinated by the world around them. This kitten was no exception and ladybugs provided endless entertainment for him. The design is repeated so that it can be viewed from both sides. However, if you prefer to stitch it once, you can use the other half to add your name or initials or date. Whichever option you choose, this delightful kitten is bound to brighten up your coffee hour.

MATERIALS

For design, stitched area of 1 side 4¾ x 3⅝ in
   (12 x 9 cm)

Zweigart 14-count Aida cloth in cream,
   17 x 10 in (43 x 25.5 cm)

DMC Six Strand Embroidery Floss as follows:

712	Pale Cream
739	Cream Beige
3827	Pale Ginger
436	Light Caramel
976	Dark Ginger
435	Dark Caramel
838	Dark Brown
817	Red
350	Geranium Red
3712	Dark Rose Pink
743	Yellow
472	Pale Green
471	Medium Green
3346	Dark Green

Tapestry needles, size 24

Satin bias binding, approximately 1 yd or 1 m
   in coffee or red

Lightweight batting, approximately 17 x 10 in
   (43 x 25.5 cm)

Backing fabric: linen, Aida cloth or lightweight
   wool, 17 x 10 in (43 x 25.5 cm)

Thread for basting

Cotton thread for bias binding and Velcro

Length of hook and loop Velcro, 10 in
   (25.5 cm), in a suitable color (pink was
   used in the piece illustrated)

WORKING THE CROSS STITCH

Fold the Aida in half to find the midpoint of
the two design areas. Following the chart,
work the design beginning at the right-hand
edge of the design, four holes to the left of the
center fold. Work the repeat of the design,
beginning at the left-hand edge, four holes to
the right of the center fold. (The design and
repeat are therefore eight holes apart along
the length of the Aida cloth.) Work French
knots in colors specified below.

Five French knots in 743 on upper small
strawberry
Four French knots in 743 on lower small
strawberry

First ladybug:	Four French knots in 838
	Two French knots in 712
Second ladybug:	Two French knots in 838
	Two French knots in 712

*Use three strands for all the cross stitch areas.
Use one strand for all the French knots. (See
Getting Started page 13 for details on how to
work French knots.)*

FINISHING THE WORK

See *Finishing Your Work* page 123 for details
on finishing your coffeepot cover.

ALTERNATIVE SUGGESTIONS
FOR THE DESIGN

A single working of the design would be
suitable for a small picture or calendar, using
an oval or rectangular mount. A slightly larger
picture, measuring 6 x 4½ in (15.5 x 11.5 cm)
can be created by working the design on
11-count Aida cloth. (Remember to allow for
the increase in size when calculating the
amount of Aida required.)

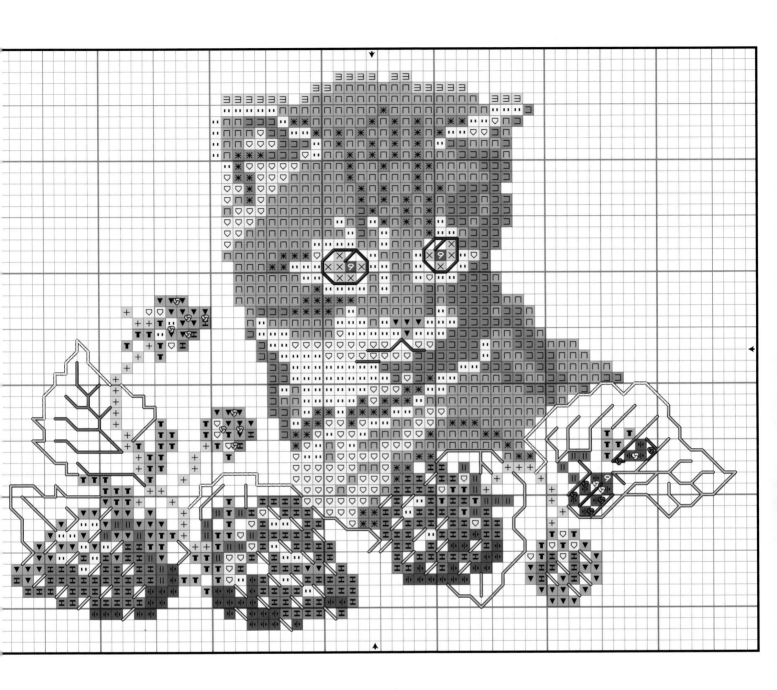

Key

DMC numbers
underlined
indicates
backstitch

Symbol	DMC		Symbol	DMC		Symbol	DMC		Symbol	DMC		Symbol	DMC
⊙··	712		⊓	436		♥9	838		▼	3712		T	471
♡	739		✳	976		·◖·	817		+⊙	743		‖	3346
Ⅎ	3827		⊐	435		⊟	350		✕	472			

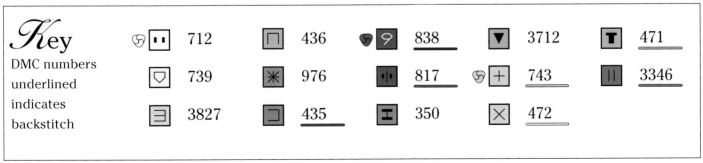

Mini-sampler

Stitch this mini-sampler as a gift for your favorite cat lover or even yourself. In a bedroom, this piece will bring a smile to a visitor's face and make your guest feel immediately at home.

MATERIALS

For design, stitched area 5¾ x 3⅞ in
   (14.5 x 10 cm)

Zweigart 28-count linen in cream,
   12 x 10 in (30.5 x 25.5 cm)

Six Strand Embroidery Floss as follows:

310	Black
B5200	White
799	Blue
453	Pale Gray
642	Medium Gray
3787	Dark Gray
838	Dark Brown
841	Coffee
3033	Mushroom
3827	Pale Ginger
976	Ginger
349	Red
3046	Pale Gold
471	Green

Tapestry needles, size 24

Frame, internal measurement 6¾ x 4⅜ in
   (16 x 11 cm)

WORKING THE CROSS STITCH

Follow the chart, beginning at the center of
the linen and working outward.

*Two strands are worked over two canvas
threads with the following exceptions:
The gray paw prints are worked in one strand
over one canvas thread.
The "sleeping" cat's eyes and nose are worked
in one strand over one and two canvas threads.*

FINISHING THE WORK

See *Finishing Your Work* page 122 for details
on how to prepare your work for framing and
other framing information.

ALTERNATIVE SUGGESTIONS FOR THE DESIGN

Various elements of the sampler can be used
to decorate small items. For example, make a
set of cat buttons to personalize a cardigan,
sweater, or jacket.

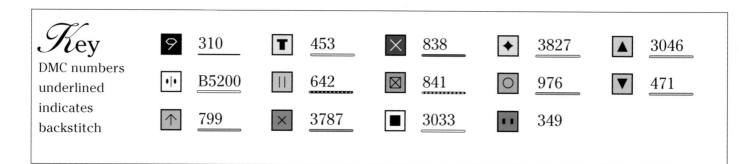

Key
DMC numbers
underlined
indicates
backstitch

℔ 310	T 453	⊠ 838	◆ 3827	▲ 3046
⋅	⋅ B5200	‖ 642	⊠ 841	○ 976	▼ 471
↑ 799	✕ 3787	■ 3033	⦂⦂ 349	

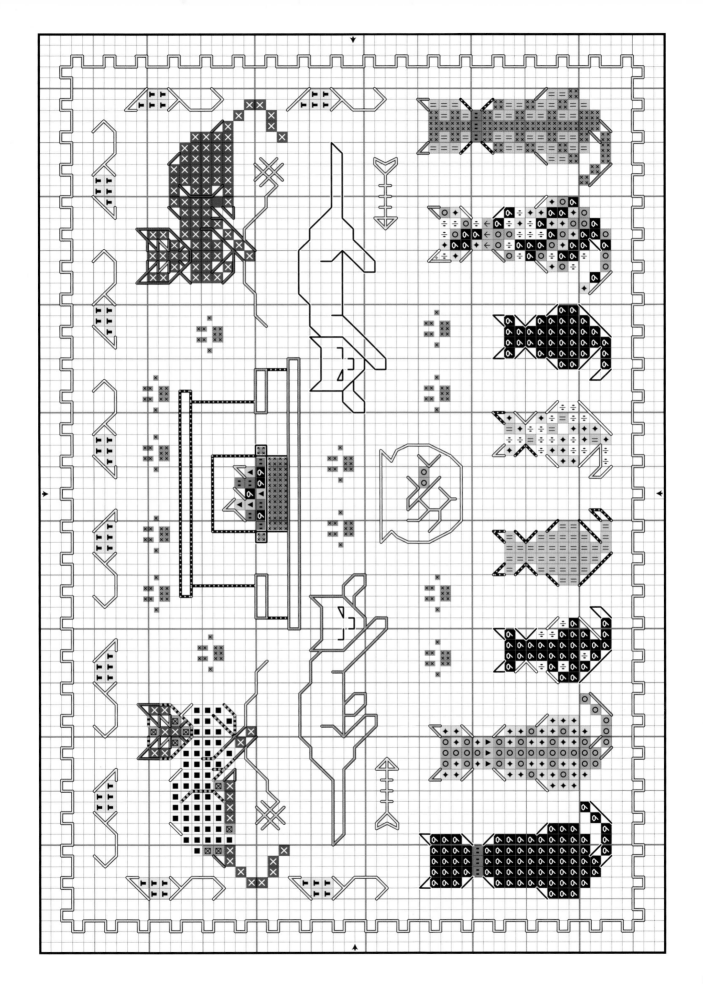

Plant Mat

On a sunny day cats often like to hide
in a cool spot, *after* sunbathing of course, and
ivy provides excellent cover. This has been
designed for use as a mat for a plant on
a low table. However, it can also be used
on a shelf with the triangular design
overhanging the shelf edge.

MATERIALS

For design, stitched area 8⅜ (21.5 cm) square

Zweigart 14-count Aida cloth in white, 9¾ in (24.5 cm) square

DMC Six Strand Embroidery Floss as follows:

760	Dark Pink
453	Mink
948	Pale Pink
762	Pale Gray
648	Medium Gray
646	Dark Gray
844	Mud
935	Darkest Green
987	Dark Green
3347	Medium Green
472	Lime green
834	Gold
543	Cream
BLANC	White

Tapestry needles, size 24

Satin bias binding, 40 in (1 m), in dark green

Cotton thread to match bias binding

WORKING THE CROSS STITCH

Before starting the cross stitch, attach the bias binding to construct the mat. Begin and end the bias binding at one corner of the Aida. You will probably find that you have three rounded corners and one square corner. Begin to work the cross stitch opposite the square corner. The corner motif will be seven rows in from the inner edges of the binding. Place the corner motif in each corner and rotate at 90°.

Follow the chart, working the cat first and then each of the ivy sprigs.

Use two strands for the cat and ivy leaves. Use one strand for the backstitch outlining the leaves.

FINISHING THE WORK

Press with a damp cloth and a medium-hot iron on the reverse side of the fabric.

ALTERNATIVE SUGGESTIONS FOR THE DESIGN

This design can be worked on an oblong piece of fabric to create a tray cloth. For this use, the design should be worked in two opposite corners. Another idea is to use it for the square tray on page 98.

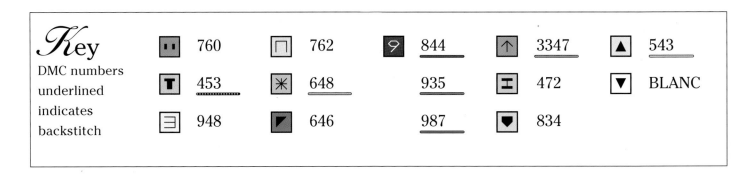

Key

DMC numbers underlined indicates backstitch

▪▪ 760	⊓ 762	9 844	↑ 3347	▲ 543	
T 453	✳ 648	935	⊟ 472	▼ BLANC	
⊒ 948	◩ 646	987	◆ 834		

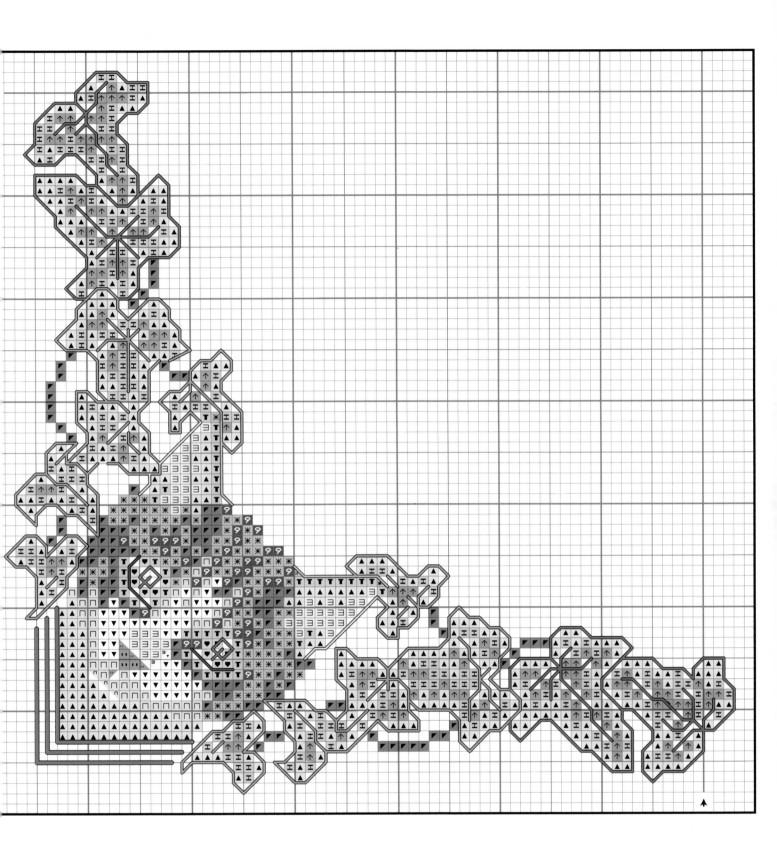

Photograph Album Cover

This design uses the half-Persian cat featured on the wooden needles and scissors box. The border is intentionally simple so that it can be extended or adapted to accommodate different sized photograph albums. You can also use it to cover a diary, sketch book, or other small book.

MATERIALS

For design, stitched area 5½ x 3¾ in
 (14 x 9.5 cm)

Zweigart 14-count Aida cloth in black,
 9 x 15 in (23 x 38 cm)

DMC Medicis Wool as follows:

BLANC   White
8739   Buttermilk
8846   Pale Ginger
8845   Ginger
8301   Dark Ginger
8166   Dusty Pink
8742   Gold
8420   Green

Tapestry needles, size 22
Black cotton thread
Photograph album
Double-faced adhesive tape

WORKING THE CROSS STITCH

Begin with either the tip of the cat's tail or the bottom left-hand corner of the outer border, positioning your stitching ½ in (1.5 cm) from the corner of the book. To find where the corner will be on the Aida cloth, wrap the fabric around the book like a loose-leaf cover, ensuring that both ends tucked inside the album's front and back covers are similar in length. Also check that you have the other two edges matching each other in length. Find the bottom left-hand corner and mark with either chalk or a pin. Remove the Aida cloth from the book and begin stitching ½ in (1.5 cm) both up and across from the pin.

Use one strand of Medicis wool throughout.

FINISHING THE WORK

Photograph albums vary in size so you will need to adapt the cover to your particular album as follows:

Place the stitched area in the center of the front cover. Wrap the rest of the fabric around the back of the album. Trim the edges which will form the pockets for the covers so that you have 2 in (5 cm) for the inside of each cover end. Trim the other edges which are at right angles to the pockets, allowing ⅜ in (1 cm) for each hem. Use double-sided tape for these edges and fold under to create a neat edge. To make the pockets, turn the edges under ⅜ in (1 cm), then turn again to create a pocket approximately 1½ in (3.5 cm) deep. Slip stitch to secure the edges of the pockets. Fit to the album.

ALTERNATIVE SUGGESTIONS FOR THE DESIGN

Apart from the suggestion for this design made in the wooden needles and scissors box, it can also be used as a repeat motif for the calico bag panel on page 90. It can be worked three times with suitable spacing or you can also work the design twice in the space, reversing one of the motifs, so that you have two cats looking at each other.

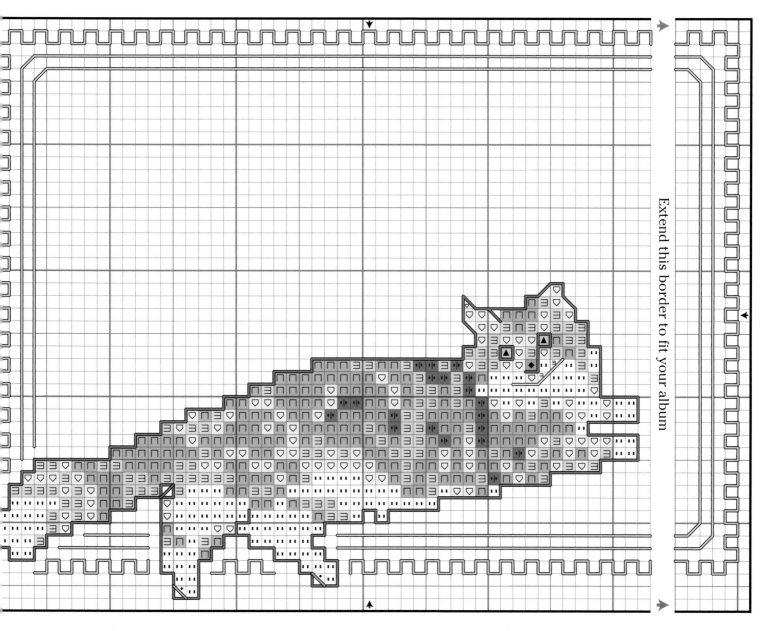

Extend this border to fit your album

Key

DMC numbers underlined indicates backstitch

⚏ BLANC	☰ <u>8846</u>	⬗ <u>8301</u>	▲ 8742 Gold
▽ 8739	⊓ 8845	◆ 8166	<u>8420</u>

Wall-hanging

Juliet is fond of sitting in a variety of inappropriate containers – everything from a laundry basket to the hanging basket shown here. Like most cats she prefers to rest in a discarded cardboard box rather than a specially designed cat bed.

MATERIALS

For design, stitched area 4¼ x 7⅝ in
   (11 x 19.5 cm)

Zweigart 14-count Aida cloth in white,
   9 x 15 in (23 x 38 cm)

DMC Six Strand Embroidery Floss as follows:

310	Black
3799	Charcoal
762	Pale Gray
BLANC	White
3823	Cream
3820	Gold
3772	Rose Brown
758	Blush
951	Flesh
957	Pink
892	Pink Red
553	Violet
340	Bluebell
113	Variegated Blue
3053	Sage Green
703	Bright Green
472	Lime Green
470	Green
831	Moss

Tapestry needles, size 24
Bell-pull hardware
Iron-on backing fabric
Double-faced adhesive tape

WORKING THE CROSS STITCH

Follow the chart, beginning in the center of the Aida and working outward.

Use two strands throughout.

FINISHING THE WORK

Carefully iron the back of your work to remove all creases. Use a medium-hot iron and a damp cloth. Position the backing fabric on the back of your work, adhesive side down, and iron. When cool, trim the finished piece to size, remembering to leave ⅜ in (1 cm) for each side hem and 1 in (2.5 cm) top and bottom for the bell-pull ends. Fix double-faced tape to the side edges and make a hem. Do the same at the top and bottom edges but make a hem 2 in (5 cm) deep, leaving space to slide the bell-pull ends into position.

ALTERNATIVE SUGGESTIONS FOR THE DESIGN

This can be framed as a picture. If you want to do something more elaborate, use it as a center panel for a small cushion.

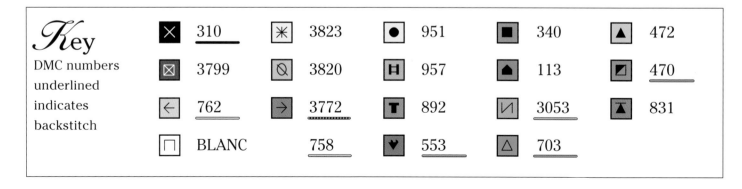

Key

DMC numbers underlined indicates backstitch

☒	310	✳	3823	●	951	■	340	▲	472
⊠	3799	◓	3820	H	957	▲	113	◪	470
←	762	→	3772	T	892	⩘	3053	▼	831
▢	BLANC		758	♥	553	△	703		

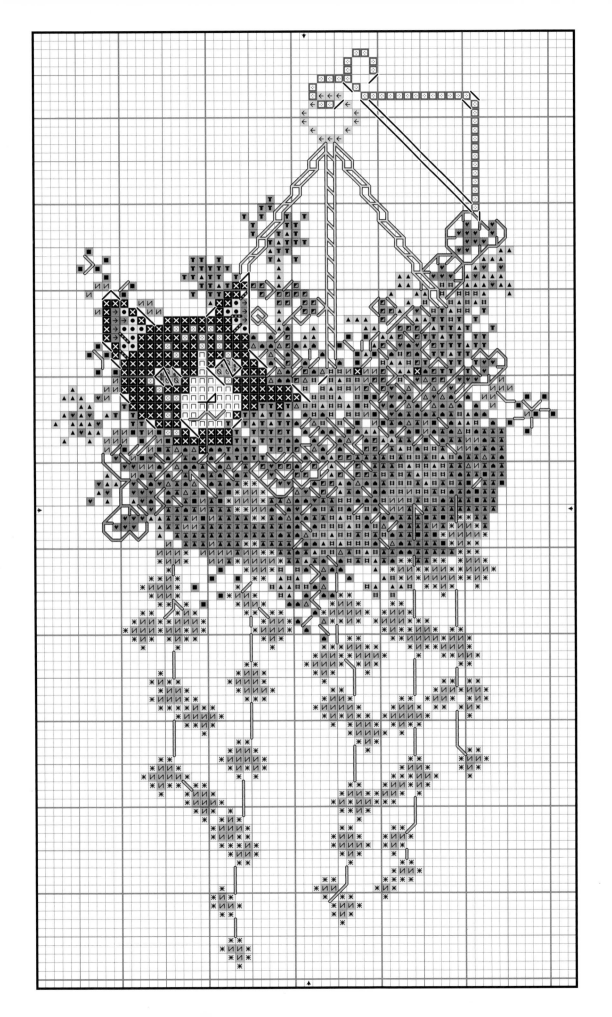

Calico Bag

This bag can be used for a variety of purposes. Rainbow colors have been used for the design so that it will fit in with most kitchen color schemes. Of course, it can always be used to carry home your cat food!

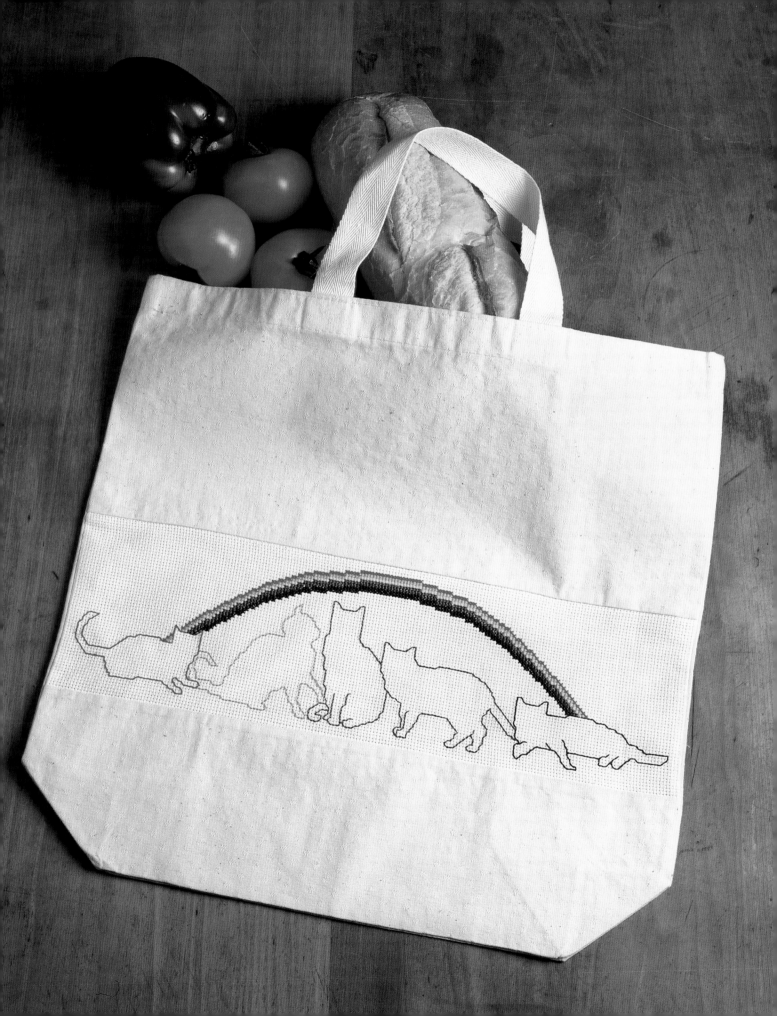

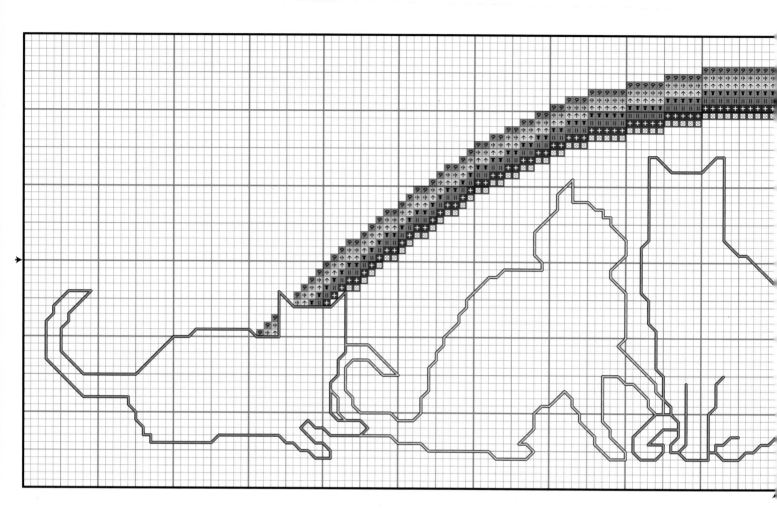

MATERIAL

For design, stitched area 13½ x 3¾ in
   (34.5 x 9.5 cm)

Canvas bag with Aida cloth insert

DMC Six Strand Embroidery Floss as follows:

606	Red
741	Orange
726	Yellow
905	Green
798	Blue
791	Indigo
550	Violet

Tapestry needles, size 24

WORKING THE CROSS STITCH

The chart is split down the midpoint of the
Aida panel. Begin the midpoint of the rainbow
on this line, leaving three clear rows of Aida
from the top edge of the panel to the first
stitch of the red in the rainbow.

Use two strands throughout.

FINISHING THE WORK

Iron the bag inside out, using a damp cloth
and a medium-hot iron.

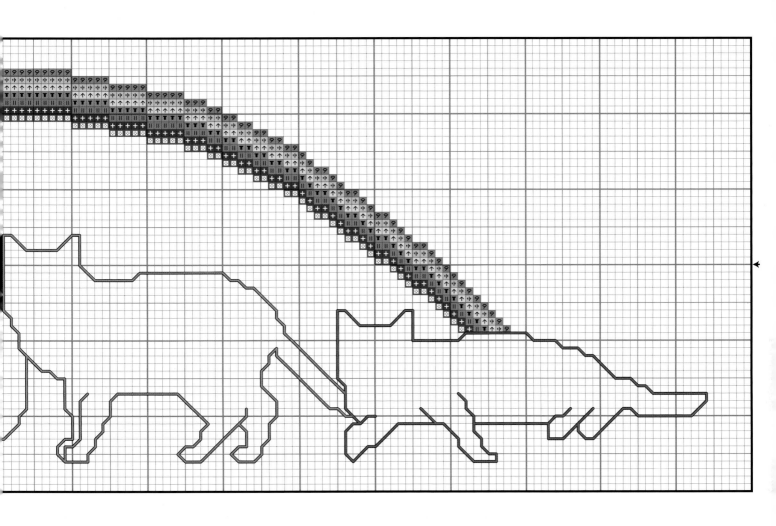

ALTERNATIVE SUGGESTIONS FOR THE DESIGN

This can be framed as a picture to brighten up a nursery or a child's bedroom. The individual cat outlines can also be used to decorate a variety of small items.

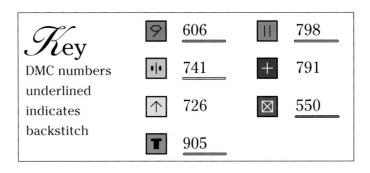

Key
DMC numbers
underlined
indicates
backstitch

606	798
741	791
726	550
905	

Clock

These three rescued cats all have an owner in common but you can substitute your own cat or cats for any or all of them in the design of this pretty clock.

MATERIALS

For design, stitched area 4¼ x 6⅛ in
  (11 x 15.5 cm)

Zweigart 14-count Aida cloth in white,
  10 x 14 in (25.5 x 35.5 cm)

DMC Six Strand Embroidery Floss as follows:

310	Black
3799	Dark Gray
3371	Dark Brown
3021	Medium Brown
746	Cream
BLANC	White
3779	Pink
972	Orange Yellow
444	Dark Yellow
727	Lemon
3348	Lime Green
368	Pale Apple Green
320	Apple Green
964	Turquoise Green
825	Kingfisher Blue
792	Bluebell
3746	Mauve
209	Pale Violet
552	Violet

Tapestry needles, size 24

Clock kit with embroidery insert 5 x 7 in
  (12.5 x 18 cm)

French navy aerosol spray paint

WORKING THE CROSS STITCH

The small circle of backstitch at the center of the clock should be stitched first. Follow the chart and work outward from this area.

Use two strands throughout.

FINISHING THE WORK

Spray the clock with thin coats of spray paint, allowing 24 hours between coats. Then follow the instructions provided with the clock for completing the project. See *Finishing Your Work* page 122 for details on preparing your work for framing.

ALTERNATIVE SUGGESTIONS FOR THE DESIGN

The central design can be used to decorate a box lid or to enhance the front of a covered book, such as the photograph album cover on page 82.

If you wish to substitute another cat's face for one in the design, you will need a photograph of the face which is similar in size to that in the design. Lay a piece of 14 squares per inch design paper over the top and trace the outline on to the paper. Fill in the detail from your photograph and then stitch.

Key
DMC numbers underlined indicates backstitch

▨	310	⊟	746	⊥	444	H	320	◩	3746
‖	3799	⊓	BLANC	▼	727	T	964	▾	209
••	3371	•ǀ•	3779	◆	3348	∧	825	+	552
▽	3021	✳	972	●	368	▲	792		

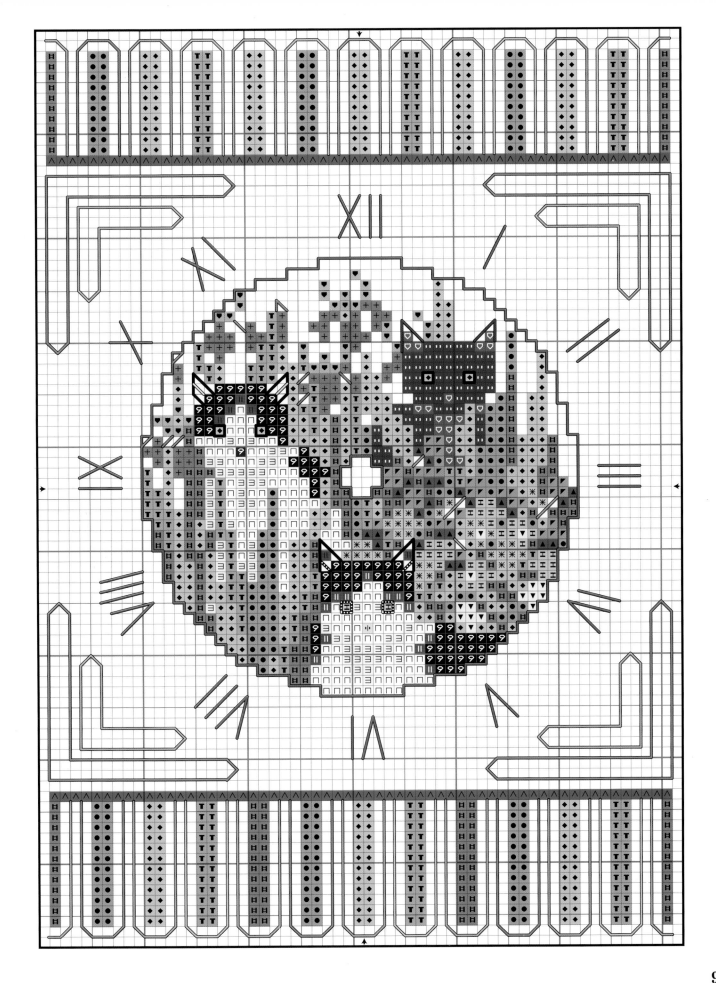

Square Tray

Penny is special and she loves her garden.
If desired, you can substitute your own cat's
face in the center of the design.

MATERIALS

For design, stitched area 8 in (20.5 cm) square

Zweigart 28-count linen in white, 15 in (38 cm) square

DMC Six Strand Embroidery Floss as follows:

The Cat

BLANC	White
677	Buttermilk
676	Dark Cream
632	Variegated Gold
402	Coffee
436	Pale Ginger
613	Ecru
3787	Mud Gray
844	Pinky beige
310	Black
3778	Pink

The Nasturtiums

471	Pale green
520	Dark green
472	Variegated Green
783	Blush
745	Pale Yellow
743	Yellow
741	Orange
947	Dark Orange
349	Red

Tapestry needles, size 24

Square tray, with embroidery insert 9 in (23 cm) square

Black aerosol spray paint

WORKING THE CROSS STITCH

Work the first corner motif 3½ in (9 cm) from the corner of the linen. Work each corner motif in turn, rotating the chart through 90° and leaving 15 stitches between the edges of the motifs. (15 stitches = 30 threads of the linen.)

Work the cat's face by finding the center of your fabric and working from the center of the chart. To substitute your own cat's face, see page 11.

Use two strands throughout.

FINISHING THE WORK

See *Finishing Your Work* page 122 for details on preparing your work for framing. Then follow the instructions provided with the tray to complete the project.

ALTERNATIVE SUGGESTIONS FOR THE DESIGN

The corner motif can be used for a tray cloth or napkins. The cat's face can be used to decorate either a teapot stand or, if stitched on 18-count Aida cloth, for a box lid.

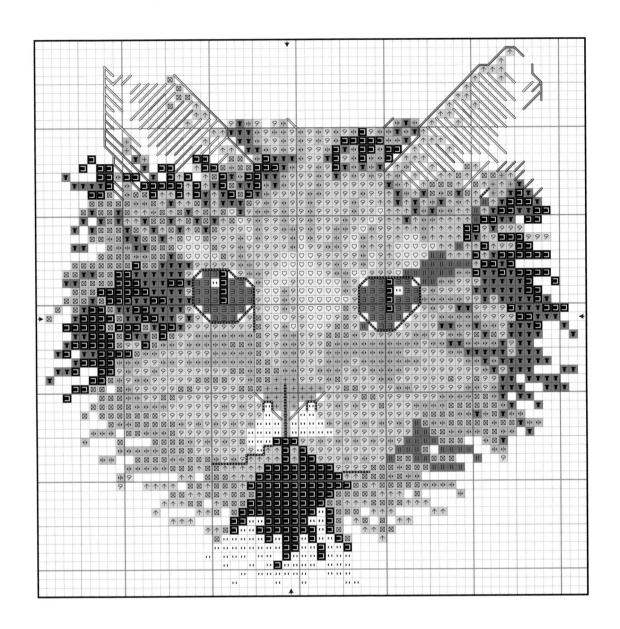

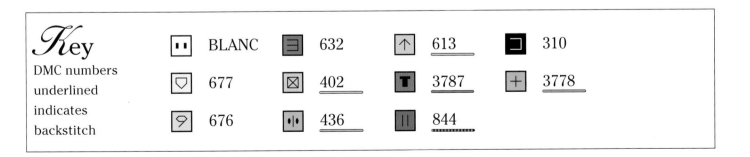

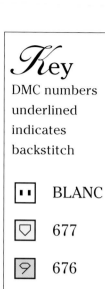

Key

DMC numbers
underlined
indicates
backstitch

⊡	BLANC
▽	677
⊘	676
☰	632
⊠	402
◖▮◗	436
↑	613
▜	3787
‖	844
◪	310
✛	3778

Above: Key for Cat

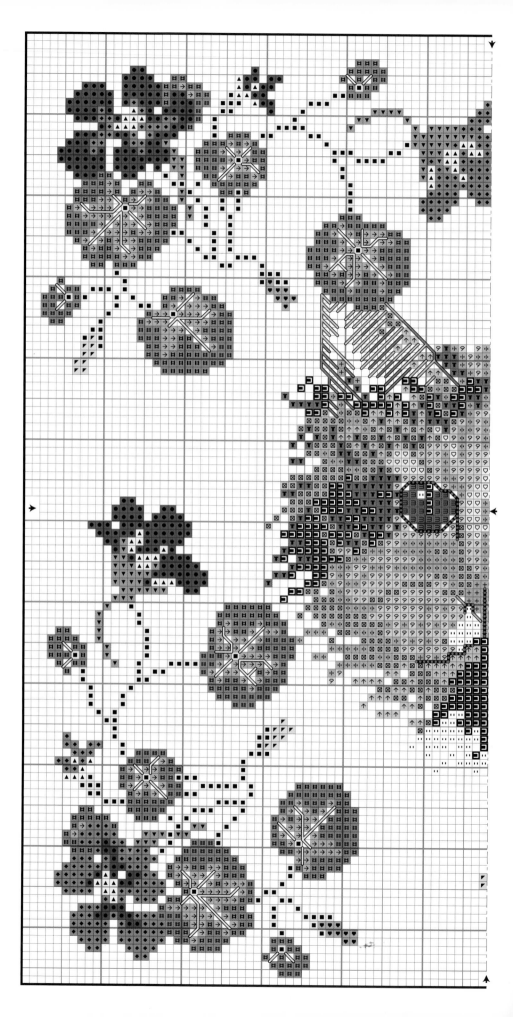

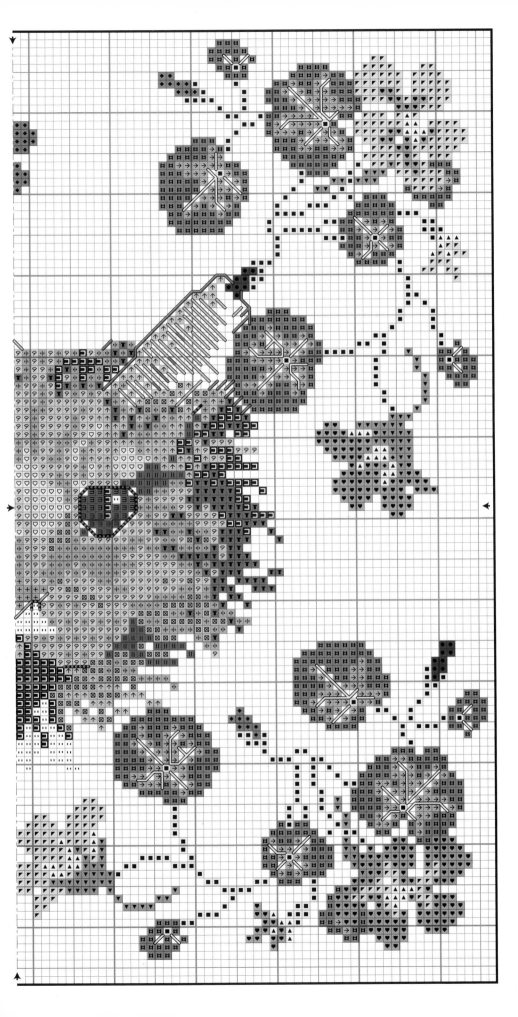

Oval Tray

Misty and Softy are glamorous cats who love to lie around looking decorative. They enjoy gardening, better described as napping in the sunny flower borders, so they are a suitable pair for this elegant floral tray. This tray has been created to say thank you to good neighbors but it would also be a suitable birthday gift or retirement present.

MATERIALS

For design, stitched area 11⅝ x 6¾ in
(30 x 17 cm)

Zweigart 25-count Dublin linen in shade 222,
18 x 13 in (46 x 33 cm)

DMC Six Strand Embroidery Floss as follows:

645	Dark Gray
647	Stone Gray
648	Gray
3072	Pale Gray
BLANC	White
760	Pink
335	Red
436	Pale Brown
834	Antique Gold
727	Yellow
472	Lime Green
471	Green
3012	Olive Green
504	Pale Turquoise
340	Mauve

Tapestry needles, size 24
Wood tray kit with embroidery insert
11⅝ x 6¾ in (30 x 17 cm)

WORKING THE CROSS STITCH

Follow the chart, beginning in the center of
the linen and working outward.

*Use three strands for everything except the gold
border and striped background, for which one
strand is used.*

FINISHING THE WORK

Follow the manufacturer's instructions for
assembling the tray.

𝒦ey
DMC numbers
underlined
indicates
backstitch

◈	645	⊟	3072	✳	335	▼	727	▼	3012
▪▪	647	⊓	BLANC	⊐	436	▲	472	◆	504
▽	648	▪|▪	760	⊥	834	◣	471	●	340

Above: Key for Embroidery Floss

ALTERNATIVE SUGGESTION FOR THE DESIGN

This design can be adapted to create a companion cushion by extending the stripes and adding a background color. The design can be worked on 10-count Tapestry Canvas (double thread would be best) in half cross stitch using wool. It will make a rectangular cushion measuring 16 x 12 in (40.5 x 30.5 cm). The recommended DMC Tapestry Wool colors are as follows:

7275	Dark Gray
7273	Stone Gray
7618	Gray
7282	Pale Gray
BLANC	White
7105	Pink
7104	Red
7846	Pale Brown
7473	Antique Gold
7078	Yellow
7584	Lime Green
7583	Green
7364	Olive Green
7322	Pale Turquoise
7711	Mauve
7746	Cream for the background

Tapestry needles, size 16

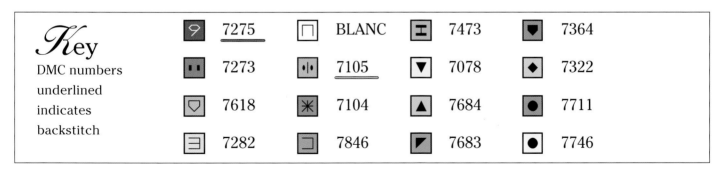

Above: Key for Tapestry Wool

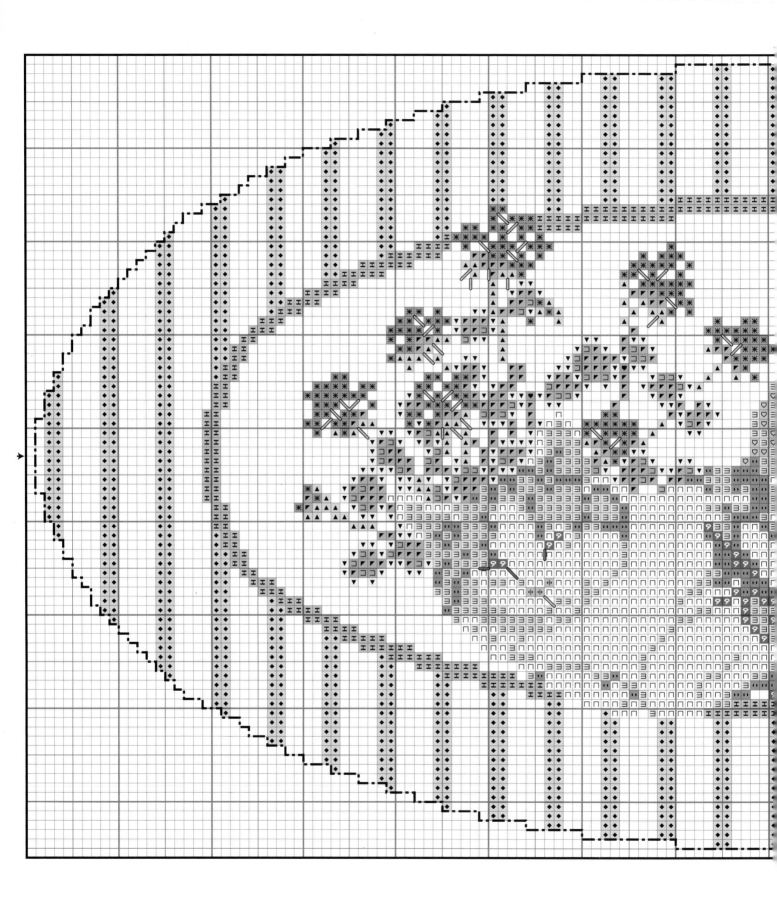

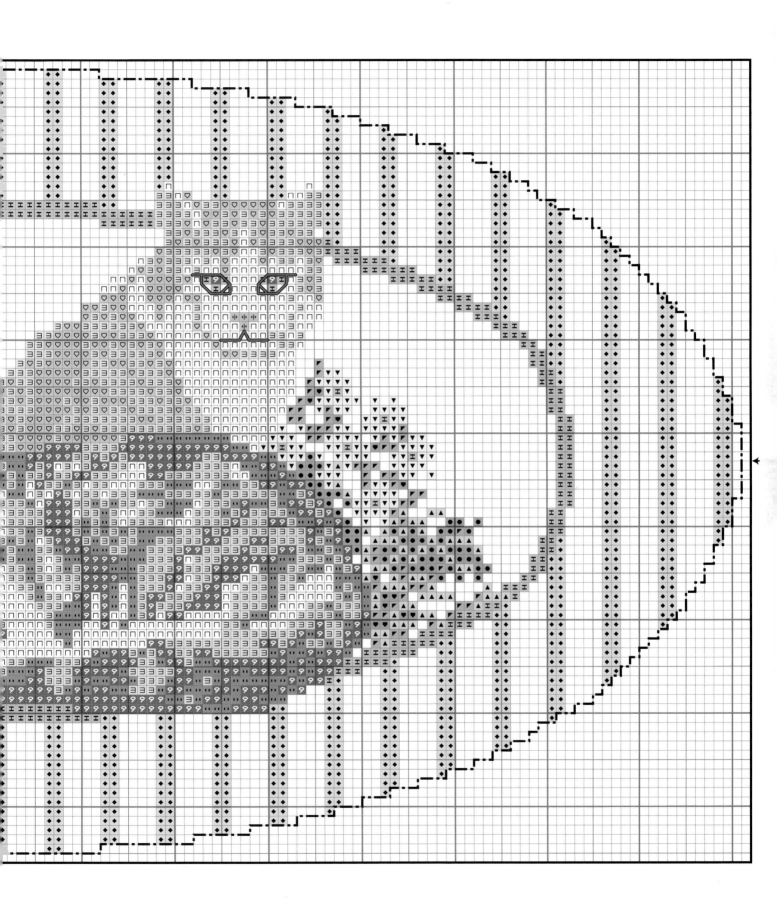

Herb Pillow

This design of a long-haired kitten is the same as that used for the mirror but is worked in a different colorway. It is also worked on smaller count fabric and, when combined with the tartan background, makes a very pretty herb pillow. The bottom edge is left open and secured with ribbons so that the herbs can easily be replenished. The colors of the tartan background can easily be changed to shades that complement colors of your room.

MATERIALS

For design, stitched area 8½ in
   (21.5 cm) square

Zweigart 14-count Aida cloth in blue (shade
   589), 14 x 28 in (35.5 x 71 cm)
DMC Six Strand Embroidery Floss as follows:

310	Black
353	Pink
422	Pale Gold
739	Pale Coffee
B5200	White
746	Rich Cream
712	Milk
822	Stone
3033	Pale Mushroom
3782	Mushroom
799	Blue
501	Sea Green
989	Green
666	Red

Tapestry needles, size 24
Cotton thread to match the Aida and ribbon
Length of blue ribbon (to match 799), 60 in
   (150 cm)
Batting
Herbs such as rosemary or thyme, or
   potpourri

WORKING THE CROSS STITCH

Along the two short edges press under a hem
allowance of ⅝ in (1.5 cm). Slip stitch both
hems. Fold the fabric in half to create the
pillow shape. Find the center of the front half
and work from the chart, beginning in the
center and working outward.

*Use all three strands for the cat. Use two strands
for the tartan and all backstitches.*

FINISHING THE WORK

Stitch the side seams of the pillow, right sides
together, using a ⅝ in (1.5 cm) seam
allowance. Turn right-side out and press the
back of the pillow and the side seams using a
damp cloth and warm iron. Cut the ribbon
into four equal lengths and attach the
ribbons, approximately 3 inches (or one-
quarter of the pillow width) in from each
edge, to the back and front bottom edges of
the pillow. Fold the batting in half so that it
fits the pillow, then insert the herbs in the
fold. Place in the pillow so that the folded
edge is at the bottom edge of the pillow. Tie
the ribbon to secure the batting in place.

ALTERNATIVE SUGGESTIONS
FOR THE DESIGN

The tartan pattern can be applied to a whole
range of items, anything from a box lid to a
book cover or a bag. The colors can be
changed to match your decor by choosing
three colors from your color scheme. Simply
decide which color should dominate and use
this instead of 666. The kitten makes a pretty
picture in its own right.

Below: Key for Kitten

𝒦ey

DMC numbers
underlined
indicates
backstitch

9	310	▽	739	✳	712	▼	3782
ı|ı	353	⊟	B5200	⊡	822	▲	799
··	422	⊓	746	⊞	3033		

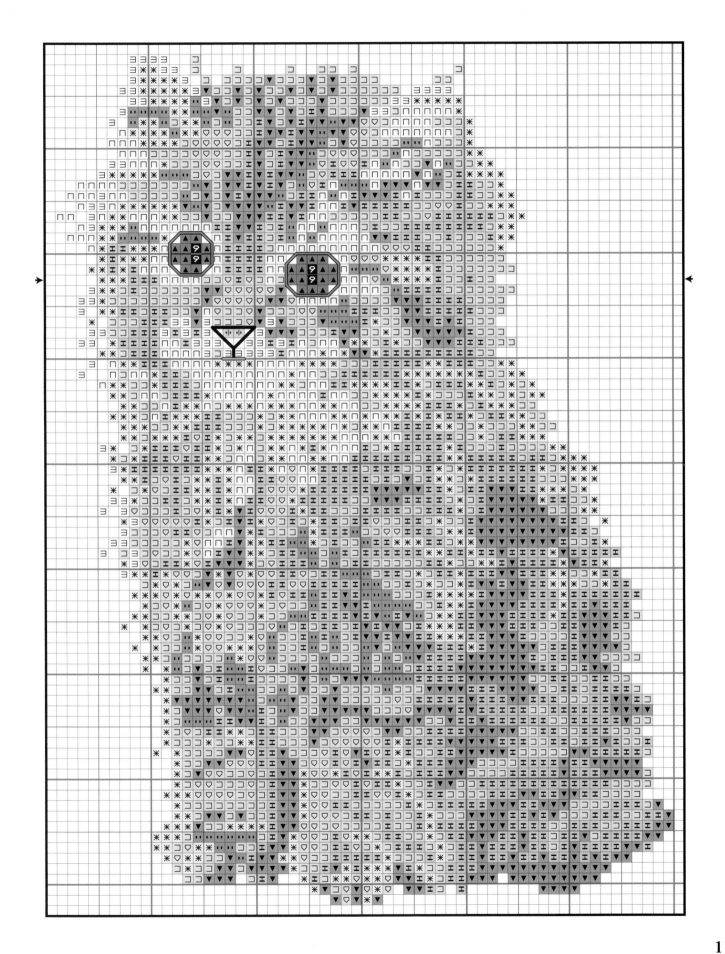

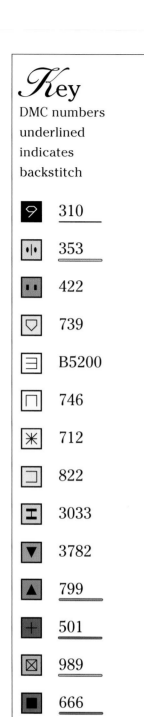

*K*ey

DMC numbers
underlined
indicates
backstitch

Symbol	Number
⊋	310
⦙	353
⦂	422
▽	739
⊟	B5200
⊓	746
✳	712
⊐	822
⊞	3033
▼	3782
▲	799
✛	501
⊠	989
■	666

Above: Key for
Background

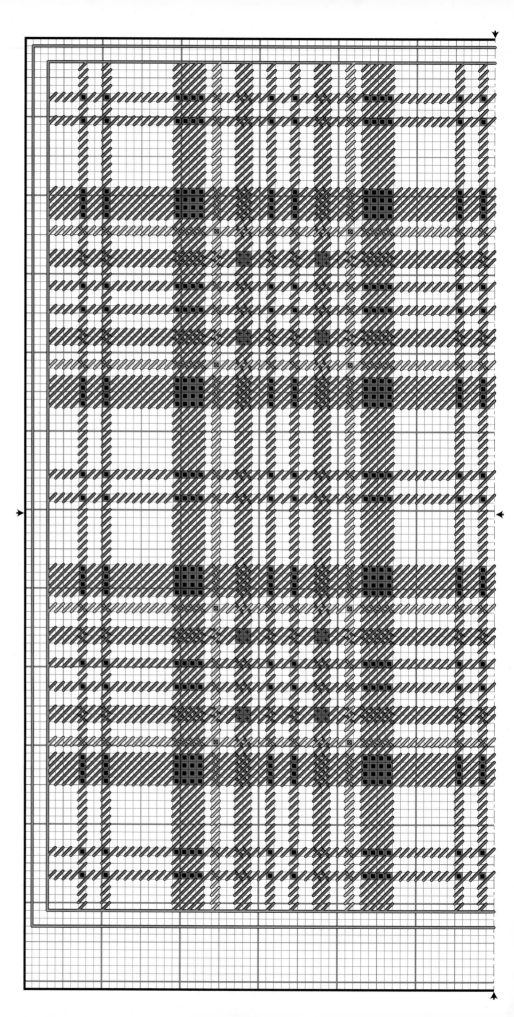

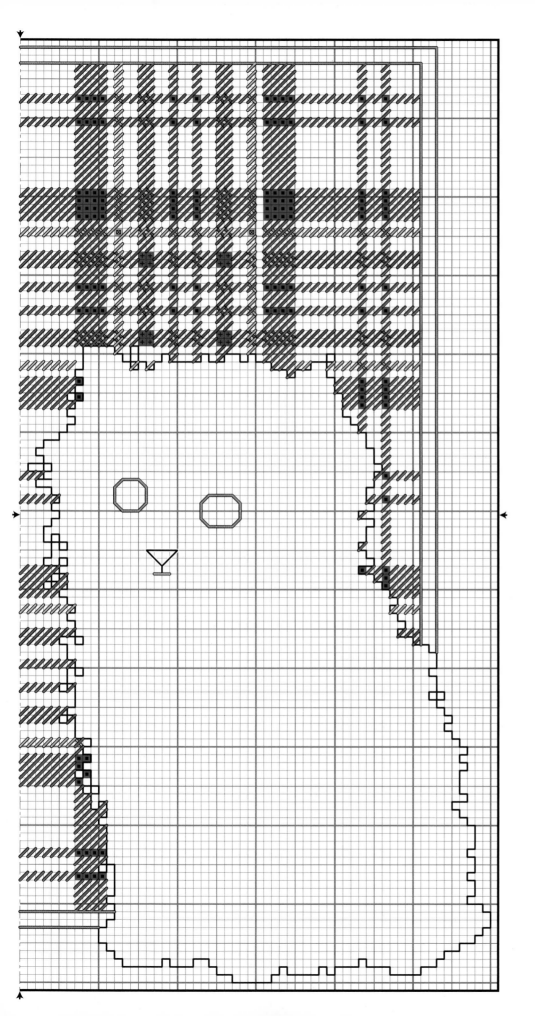

Breakfast Set

This cheery trio should put a smile on your face each morning over breakfast. The gingham border is worked in red but would look equally good in green, yellow or blue, so it can be adapted for your personal color scheme. The kittens are reduced in size for the egg cozies simply by stitching the same chart on finer fabric. Make as many egg cozies as you need; to make each one distinctive, vary the color of the single poppy on the reverse side of the cozy.

MATERIALS

For tea cozy, stitched area 12½ x 9¾ in (32 x 25 cm) and egg cozy, stitched area 3¾ x 4⅞ in (9.5 x 12.5 cm)

Zweigart 11-count Aida cloth in antique white, 18 x 14 in (46 x 36 cm) for the tea cozy

Zweigart 14-count Aida cloth in antique white, 6½ x 8 in (16.5 x 20.5 cm) for each egg cozy

DMC Six Strand Embroidery Floss as follows:

310	Black
414	Gunmetal Gray
3042	Cream
BLANC	White
727	Pale Yellow
972	Yellow
741	Pale Orange
608	Orange Red
666	Red
304	Dark Red
353	Pink
3827	Pale Gold
3776	Ginger
3782	Coffee
3787	Mud Brown
472	Lime Green
3347	Leaf Green

Tapestry needles, size 24
Batting, lining and backing fabric for the tea cozy
Batting and lining for the egg cozies
Cotton thread
Bias binding in color to match the gingham border
Air-soluble marker

Below: Key for Back of Egg Cozy

WORKING THE CROSS STITCH

Follow the charts, beginning in the center of the Aida and working outward.

Use three strands for the tea cozy and two strands for the egg cozies.

FINISHING THE WORK

Following the curved shape indicated on the charts and using an air-soluble marker, mark the top edge of the cozy. Make a sandwich of the layers as follows:

> Cozy front, right side up
> Batting
> Two pieces of lining fabric
> Batting
> Cozy back, right side down

Baste the layers together, ready for stitching. Stitch through all the layers beginning at the side edge of the gingham border and continue around to the other edge, following your marked line and leaving the bottom edge open. Trim the seam to ¼ in (0.6 cm) and attach the bias binding to the seam stitching. If you wish to add a ribbon loop at the center top of the cozies, position one end in place, adding it to the fabric sandwich. Attach the other end when hemming the bias binding. Attach bias binding to the bottom edge of the cozy so that the binding is at the bottom edge of the gingham pattern. Trim the seam and hem the binding.

ALTERNATIVE SUGGESTIONS FOR THE DESIGN

The kitten images can be used for greetings cards as can the central design with the adult cat. They can also be adapted to make an attractive picture, if stitched on 18-count Aida.

𝒦ey
DMC numbers underlined indicates backstitch

✳	727	⊞	741	◖◗	3787	▜	3347
⊐	972	𝟵	666	⊞	472		

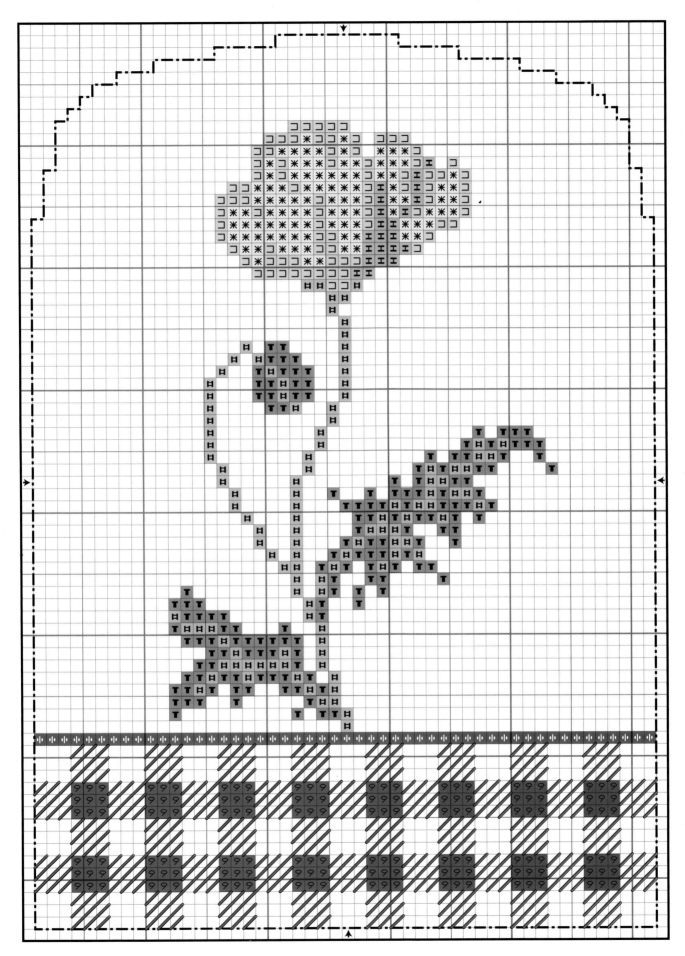

Back of Egg Cozy

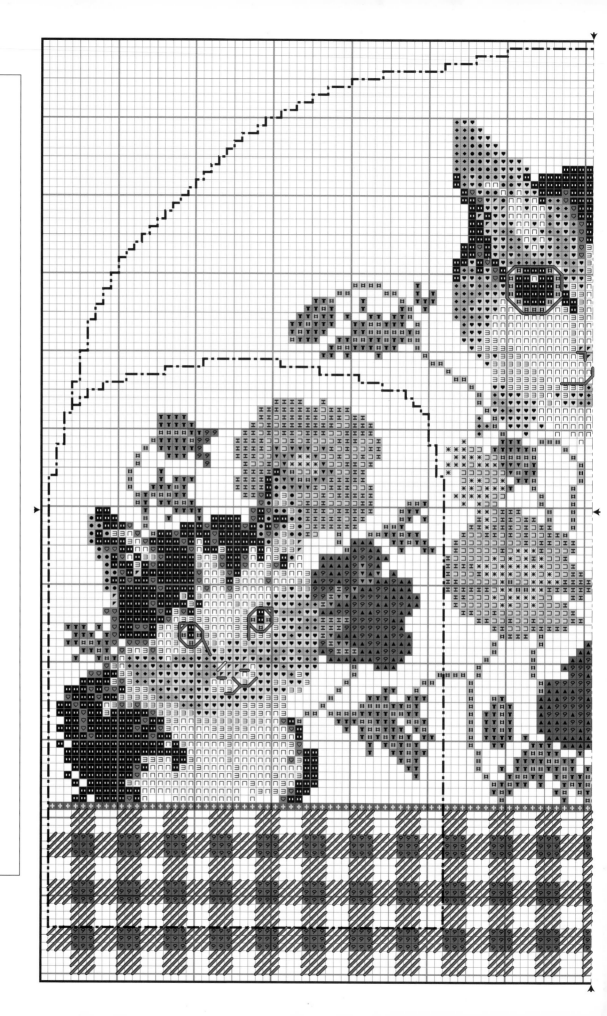

Key

DMC numbers
underlined
indicates
backstitch

■■	<u>310</u>
▽	414
ⲷ	712
⊓	BLANC
✳	727
⊐	972
⊞	741
▼	<u>608</u>
9	<u>666</u>
▲	304
◢	<u>353</u>
▼	3827
◆	3776
●	3782
◖◗	<u>3787</u>
H	472
T	3347

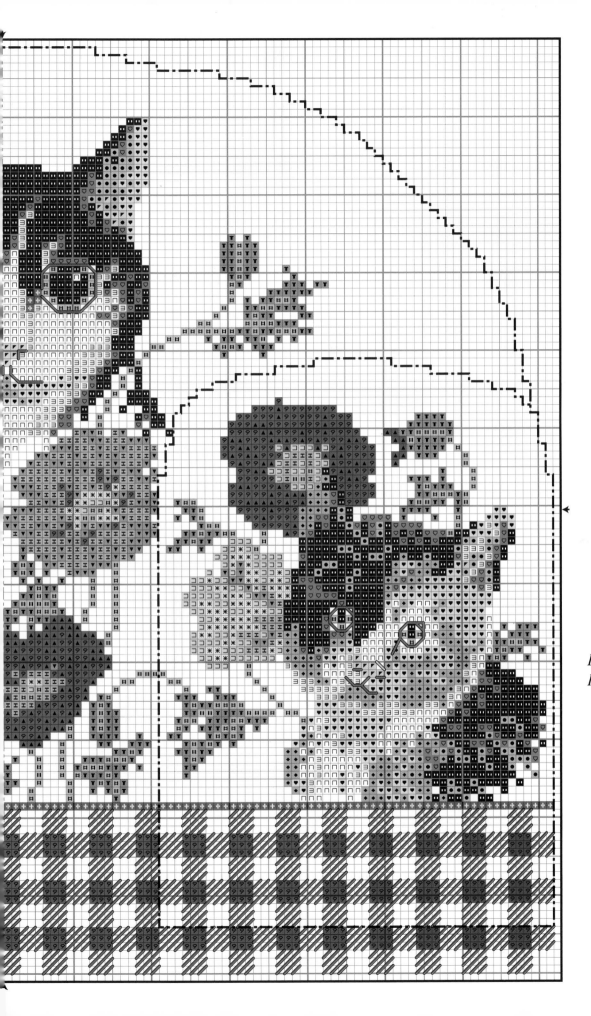

Left: Tea Cozy and
Front of Egg Cozy

121

Finishing Your Work

Remove your finished piece from the hoop or frame if you have used one. Trim any excess lengths of thread you may have left at the back of your stitching. Examine the unstitched areas and check they have remained clean. If they have not, use a specially-formulated soap, available from most good needlework retailers, and wash your work following the manufacturer's instructions. When it is dry, carefully iron the reverse side of your work using a damp cloth and a medium-hot iron. Trim the fabric to the required size (for further information, see below).

FITTING WORK TO AN OVAL

(Greeting Card, Address Book, Wooden Needles and Scissors Box)

An easy way to do this is to use a piece of tracing paper as a guide. Cut a piece of tracing paper to fit the card, book or oval area to be covered. When in position, trace the outline of the oval with pencil. Remove the tracing paper and place it over your stitched pieces, locating the design in the center of the drawn oval. Pin to the fabric and trim the fabric to fit the paper. Remove the pins and fit to the finished item. For the greeting card (page 24), use double-faced adhesive tape to secure the item in position. For the address book (page 32), carefully slide the work into position in the front cover. For the wooden needles and scissors box (page 44), use doublefaced tape to secure the fabric to the back of the cardboard insert and then use tape again to secure it to the top of the box. (See the section below for creating a second oval – or circle.)

FITTING WORK TO A CIRCLE

(Paperweight, Silver-plated Box, Pen Holder, Teapot Stand)

Use the same approach with tracing paper described above, but bear in mind that the circle you draw will most likely be the size of your finished item. You can still use this to centralize the design but will need to draw another circle outside this as a guide for trimming the fabric to a circular shape. (A plate or saucer can be used for this purpose.) Remember to leave sufficient fabric to tuck under the lid or backing of the silver-plated box (page 48), the pen holder (page 56) and the teapot stand (page 60). The paperweight (page 36) will not have any hem or fabric to tuck behind and will need to be cut to the exact size of the paperweight's inner edge. Full manufacturer's instructions are provided for the fitting of the work to each of the purchased items.

Preparing Work for Framing

(Calendar, Candlescreen, Mirror, Clock, Square Tray, Mini-sampler)

All the above projects can be prepared for framing using the following method. However, for the clock (page 94), full instructions are provided with the purchased clock kit.

Use the same approach with tracing paper as described in *Fitting Work to an Oval*, above, but make the paper the same size as the backing board. Do not trim the fabric at this stage. Use the paper to locate the design in the appropriate place. In the case of the calendar (page 28), remember to leave space for fixing the calendar blank. Pin the paper to the design. Place the fabric onto the board, matching the edges of the paper to the edges of the board. You can either begin to secure the fabric to the board by placing pins into the top and bottom edges of the board or by using double-faced adhesive tape fixed to the back of the board. After securing the top and bottom edges, continue to use the fabric threads as a guide to securing the side edges. If you find the fabric at the back of the board a little bulky, you can trim it. Fold the turned fabric neatly and fold in the corners. The final stage is to lace the opposite edges to each other using an under-and-over stitch. (If you used pins, remove them before placing the work in a frame.)

Other Framing Information

For the candlescreen (page 40) and the mirror (page 52), the frames have been used as supplied. The calendar frame (page 28) was chosen to reflect a room's decor. However, the clock (page 94) and square tray (page 98) have been re-sprayed using aerosol paint. You can use spray paint and other forms of decoration to brighten up frames. You can also glue paper around an entire frame. Colored textured paper is very good for this purpose. This suggestion is made because too often pieces of work are mounted by professional framers in dark, drab frames, so seize the opportunity to do something a little different to enhance your work.

Cushion-making

(Picture and Cushion)

Carefully press the back of your work with a damp cloth and a warm iron. Trim the tapestry canvas to leave a ½ in (1 cm) border for the seam. Cut your backing fabric to the same size. Place the right sides together and use basting stitches to secure the two pieces. Machine stitch the top and two sides of the cushion. Remove the basting stitches from the bottom edge and turn the cushion right side out. Make the tassels (four small ones for the top edge and four larger ones for the bottom). Wind a good length of red yarn round a piece of card. To finish, secure one end with a second piece of yarn. Slice the yarn along the bottom edge. Attach the tassels to the cushion. Press the seam allowance on the bottom edge, place the cushion pad inside the cushion and close up the bottom edge with small invisible slipstitches.

Coffeepot Cover

Make a sandwich of stitched work, batting, and backing fabric. Secure the outer edges with basting stitches. Attach the satin bias binding to the right side of your work to create an outer edge suitable for the size of your coffeepot. Trim the sandwich to ¼ in (0.5 cm) of your bias binding stitch line. Hem the bias binding with tiny slip stitches. Attach the Velcro strips to the inside of the cover. Place the cover around the coffeepot and trim off any excess Velcro.

Acknowledgements

Writing a book, although a seemingly solitary exercise, is always a combined effort in a variety of ways. The inspiration for the book was the BBC TV's *Animal Hospital* program in which Rolf Harris introduced viewers to the work of the Royal Society for the Prevention of Cruelty to Animals (RSPCA) Hospital and Rescue Services. The head of the veterinary staff at the Harold Harmsworth Memorial Hospital in England (where the programs were filmed) is David Grant, who has kindly written a *Foreword* for the book, and I would like to thank him and all his staff for being the inspiration behind the project and for doing such valuable work.

For their more "hands-on" involvement, I would like to thank Fran Huxley who liaised on behalf of the RSPCA, David Roberts and Sally Potter of Michael O'Mara Books, and, of course, Doreen Montgomery. For their wonderful practical assistance my thanks go to Cara Ackerman of DMC Creative World, Sarah Gray of Framecraft Miniatures, Lora Verner Designs, and John Jay and his staff. Rebecca, Tess, Sue and Jean have all made major contributions and the magazine, *All About Cats* has also played a part as have Tony and Margaret. Two final mentions and thank you's go to Susan Shanks, for continuing to promote my work in magazines, and to Peter Rogers.

Suppliers

DMC PRODUCTS

The DMC Corporation
Port Kearny,
Building 10,
South Kearny, NJ 07032
Tel (201) 589-0606
Fax (201) 589-8931

FOR FRAMECRAFT PRODUCTS

Anne Brinkley Designs Inc.
12 Chestnut Hill Lane,
Lincroft, NJ 07738
Tel (908) 530-5432
Fax (908) 530-3899

Gay Bowles Sales Inc.
P. O. Box 1060,
Janesville, WI 53547
Tel (608) 754-9212
Fax (608) 754-0665

Conversion Table
For Six Strand Embroidery Floss

This conversion table should only be used as a guide as it is not always possible to provide exact comparisons. Nearest equivalent shades are marked*.

DMC	Anchor	DMC	Anchor	DMC	Anchor	DMC	Anchor	DMC	Anchor
BLANC	2	453	231	733	280*	892	28	3042	870
ECRU	387	470	267*	738	361	893	41	3045	888
B5200	1	471	266*	739	366	902	897*	3046	887
94	1216	472	253*	741	304	904	258	3053	858*
111	1243	501	878	742	303	905	257	3072	847*
113	1210	503	875*	743	302	906	256*	3346	267*
209	109	504	1042	744	301	920	1002	3347	266*
210	108	523	859*	745	300	921	884*	3348	264
304	1006	535	1041*	746	275	931	1034	3364	260*
310	403	543	933	758	9575*	934	862*	3371	382
315	1019*	550	101	760	1022	935	861	3609	85
318	399	552	99	761	1021	947	330	3712	1023
320	215	553	98	762	234	948	1011	3746	1030
333	119	606	335	772	259	950	4146	3768	779
334	977	608	332*	775	128	951	1010	3772	1007
335	38	611	898	791	178	957	50*	3776	1048
340	118	613	831	792	941	964	185	3778	1013
341	117	640	903*	793	176	972	298	3779	868
349	13*	642	392	798	131	973	297	3782	388
350	11*	644	830	799	136	976	1001	3787	393*
353	6	645	273	807	168*	977	1002	3790	393*
368	214	646	8581*	817	13*	987	244	3799	236
371	854	647	1040	822	390	988	243	3801	35*
407	914	648	900	825	162*	989	242	3802	1019*
414	235	666	46	831	277*	996	433	3803	972
422	943*	676	891	833	907*	3012	844	3815	877
434	310*	677	886	834	874	3013	842	3817	875*
435	1046	703	238	838	380	3021	905	3820	306
436	1045	712	926	839	360*	3023	899*	3821	305*
437	362	725	305	840	379	3024	397	3823	386
444	290	726	295*	841	378	3031	360*	3827	363
451	233	727	293	844	1041*	3033	391	3828	943*